For Yahya

URBAN SURVIVAL
For the
YEARS AHEAD

Copyright 1999 by Shahrazad Ali

Published by
Shahrazad Ali
P.O. Box 17124
Cincinnati, OH 45217
2nd Edition 2017

Yahya Ali/John J, McFarlan,
Computer Specialist
All Rights Reserved.
No part of this book may be reproduced
or transmitted in any form by any means,
electronic or phyotocopying, mechanical,
recording, information storage or retrieval
system without permission from the
author Shahrazad Ali
Brief quotations may be used in
reviews or commentary only.

Surviving the hardships of the coming years affecting the ex-slaves.

Introduction - Description of Problem............1
CHAPTER 1..5
    Urban Survival in the "Hood"
    Your Location
    Legal Paperwork
    Get Your House in Order
    Escape/Back to Africa Choice
    Transportation Methods
CHAPTER 2..16
    Food, Storage and Preparation
    Oxygen Absorbers
    Vitamins
    Noah
    Lot
    House Plants, Furniture, Decor
    Apartment Vegetable Gardening
    Prophecies
    Dehydrated and Canned Foods
CHAPTER 3..30
    Water, Storing and Purification
    Requirements for Daily Living
    Odd Water Sources
    Sterilization Processes
    Sanitation, Bathing, Washing Clothes
    Human Waste Disposal
CHAPTER 4..37
    Electric, Light, Heat and Cooking
    Kerosene Lamps/Candles
    Generators
    Communication Choices
    Money, Banks, Gold, Silver

　　　　Dates to Watch For
　　　　Bartering
CHAPTER 5..54
　　　　Health and Medication
　　　　Survival Kit List
　　　　Proper Clothing
　　　　Eye Glasses
　　　　Medical Training
　　　　Mental Status
　　　　Emotions
　　　　Training for Children
　　　　Religious Faith
　　　　Spiritual Predictions
　　　　Security and Self Defense, 911
　　　　Lawyers
　　　　Prisoners and Jails
CHAPTER 6..67
　　　　Government Plans for the Unready
　　　　Triage
　　　　King Alfred Plan................................68
　　　　Presidential Executive Orders
　　　　Kosovo, NATO, UN, USA
　　　　Martial Law, FEMA
　　　　Concentration Camps......................85
　　　　Location of Detainment Centers........85
　　　　Government Reorganization Map.......87
CONCLUSION...88
SURVIVAL SUPPLIES Reference List............91
ORDER FORM for other books by Shahrazad Ali

*Note, this book is printed specifically in
　　large font to enable it to be read
easily and used as a reference text.*

iv

 # Introduction

As some may remember, I originally wrote this book to address the destructive potential of the Y2K computer problem. Y2K stands for the year 2000 which began midnight December 1999. The potential computer glitch problem was said to be a worldwide incident that promised to disrupt the entire civilized world. While reportedly there were a few technical problems, the entire system did NOT go down and life has proceeded as usual.

The majority of the cynical disbelieving American public completely ignored this perceived threat and continued on with their daily lives of work, sport and play.

Others of us got busy preparing for this cataclysmic event and purchased, gathered and studied how to survive when it all hit the fan. Most of us discuss on some level how this double evil society cannot exist forever. So we're always on the lookout for signs that the END is near so we can get ready. Us, special few commenced to prepare. Sales of can goods, water purifiers, extra blankets and candles soared. The busy got busier getting their heads in order to ward off the sure discomfort of living without most local, state and Federal conveniences, not to mention shopping at the Mall. It seems we modern PC citizens simply cannot conceive doing without our daily support system or being uncomfortable on any level for any extended period of time. All the generations are fast=== and expect speed in all transactions 24/7. This could be some kind of infectious impatience or merely sheer selfishness and overt assumption of self-importance - because we want everything *now.* Right now.

Far be it from us that we should prepare for hard times or harder times. We figure we've been through the worst.

What the hell else could happen? A lot. A whole lot. Perhaps we are also living under the misunderstanding that we'll always be taken care of – by our open enemy. We unemployed, uninsured, unrecognizable and unhappy but seemingly don't know what to do about it.

What are we prepared for? Inclement weather, hunger, water contamination, power failure, disease or civil war? Not even counting flood, tornado, hurricane, dust storm and snow. We have a new opportunity to exert our solidarity and do something for self at the same time. This is no march-in-the-street idea. This is a series of suggestions that may not only save our lives but inject new confidence in our ability to respond – currently lacking.

All of us don't have health care or life insurance but we can all play it forward by being prepared for the day of want.

Our recent history is not a good one. Our adults and children are forced to watch the wanton murder of our family members in streets all over the country. For older Blacks it's like somebody turned back the clock and we are subject to attack day or night like back in the old Jim Crow days – when the enemy's gangs would terrorize our communities randomly killing us at will and rarely being convicted – of anything. The feeling of being unprotected and prey for any demon with an evil eye is unknown to younger Blacks (Millennials), because they have been slightly brainwashed from pre-school/Headstart, that 'we' are all the same, color doesn't matter and it's better to forget about the past. The future is what it is. Today. Their particular future is grounded in the school-to-prison pipeline which is a catch-all for every Black student who is repeatedly disruptive in class, combative to the teacher and has a hooky-playing history. Many states have made open agreements with privately owned prisons/jails that they will help with fulfillment. These private owners/corporations demand a 90-95% occupancy rate – and the candidates are usually gathered from the surrounding communities from males to females. Our schools are undeniably unproductive in their teaching techniques used to educate children/youth who come from broken homes, guardian homes and no homes. It doesn't enter their minds that one day we could have a real food shortage. The government is rumbling now that it's a real possibility that the food stamp/SNAP program is near its end because of fraud. The people who steal the most are always charging others with stealing. Nevertheless, the end of the food stamp program is near and we will have to develop new disciplines to address the nationwide withdrawal from not being able to binge on food stamp goodies. FREE FOOD is going to end and we ought to be ready to handle not only the reduction of food but the limited choices we'll have when forced to pay cash. Our children, raised on cheap fast food, are NOT ready to handle a reduction in calories or availability of food. We have to start talking to them about famine because no matter how improbable it looks, we may possibly have to defy the ugly head of famine and want. This is visited on every continent at various times. We are not exempt from any disasters, natural or unnatural. Being unprepared leads to panic and panic leads to hysterical wrong choices. Let this not be us. Let us consider and look at alternative ways to survive. We have exposed our children to so many material things manufactured by the enemy or others from overseas. We want all of the stuff offered to us, especially all the technology. The downside of technology such as the Social Medias/Facebook/Instagram/Twitter etc. etc. has become a huge problem in our communications of all kind. And the popularized cell phones are promoting our demise. These items are expensive, has a cost that never ends and plays a crucial part in our personal relationships. The worst part of all is that they are addictive so they-to will have to be addressed regarding withdrawal because if there is no power anywhere no phone can be charged, no games can be played – unless you are prepared.

Lately we are all consumed with the election and mainly the unknown territory to be explored by the new President-Elect. We're not ready to admit it but the majority of the terrible things that have happened to us over the past 8 years prove that each president is just like the former one. We have not fared well under any of them. Yes, we have liked some more than others but they have all performed the same when it comes to us. Government led solutions have failed repeatedly in floods, tornados and hurricanes – people are left disappointed because they counted on someone else instead of self. The directions in this book do not require any 'coming together' just doing for self and family, quietly and steadily. The day of want is approaching fast and no amount of pity will be given out when that time is appointed. Get ready so you'll be ready.

Chapter 1

URBAN SURVIVAL IN THE "HOOD" (City Dwellers)

If the country goes into a calamity state, it will double the problems we already have in the 'hood. Our entrenched history of fighting and killing each other when we have disagreements, are jealous of each other, have new items or relationship issues - will explode – against each other. The cultural and educational level of each community will determine how violent or savage our behavior becomes – and how quickly it gets that way. We will most certainly be confined to our particular areas (just like during Katrina in New Orleans, many Blacks reported that the enemy used high-powered rifles to keep them isolated in certain areas to keep them from leaving their compounds to search other areas for food and water. Desperation drives borderline personalities to do irrational things that they ordinarily would not do.

Take stock of your own home area, define where the power lines are, outdoor faucets and drain systems. Check out your garages and sheds, you may have to live in them for a few days. Garages and sheds are easier to protect due to size. (More on this later). Most of us have too much junk in our basements and garages. We have purchased way more than we'll ever wear or use. Now is the time to start purging and separate the items which can be used for survival or trade for something else you may need. Check the windows of your house if it's your best fort. Make sure they can be boarded up easily; keep hammers, nails and some kind of boards in your basement or garage. Consider fencing your yard or part of it.

If you live in an apartment or condo, your situation will be different. If possible hole up in your apartment and bar the door best you can. Apartments tend to have one door for in and out and windows up off the ground. These are two advantages over a house. Apartments offer an opportunity to bond with other like families to build safety in numbers. Civil unrest is another reason for Black women to maintain a friendly/cordial relationship with a man or men groups because in a time of distress women need protection – both physical and emotional. Despite all of the big talk about independence, if there is a war outside our door, women need a man inside to fight. If there is limited food and water, women need men to help fend for them and protect whatever they have.

Men handle tools better and are physically stronger.

Areas in distress – where services are suspended and buses aren't running creates safety problems the longer these services are unavailable. Some will get on the road to seek a better location. During these times a van or truck is better transportation.

> *Note: Some information is repeated because "repeat means everything" and we seem to learn better when we read or hear something more than once.

Let's slow it down a bit. The first pages were designed to shift your brain into an unpredictable direction leaning towards basic and possibly primitive use of survival techniques. The purpose of this text is not to scare people into action, but to remind us that due to the evil being practiced daily across the nation, a government expected to be corrupt, the failing dollar, unemployed millions and the general dissatisfaction among our brethren, and based on similar circumstances historically, things are going to implode and explode at the same time – soon. Scientists have explained their reasoning, the stock market analysts say financial collision is approaching and every kind of soothsayer including Nostradamus, has commenced to describe how the world is ending – including the Bible. This world (way of life) as we know it is coming upon a change. This book suggests we get ready for hard times, not the end of time. Every civilization has a beginning, a time of discovery, enthusiasm of growth, a peak of success and then the slow decline based on the process used to build the civilization being torn down by the savage class who worship the filth of a beast life.

BEFORE IT ARRIVES
  - take stock of where you live, study your location and determine if you are in a place which you can barricade, board up, fence up to insulate yourself against the dangers of possible break-ins or fire. It is entirely probable that a few days after this thing hits, when your

neighbors or people in the community get hungry, they are going to go door-to-door looking for food or money, or people they know. And your house or apartment building may be attacked or set afire. Be sure your smoke alarms are working w/ extra batteries. Find out where your local parks or campgrounds are, check out the location of the zoo, highway rest-stops and community centers. Measure how far you are away from another spot and how long it will take you to get there. Of course many of us will expect the City, State or Federal government to provide us with a place if we are run out of our homes - for any reason. However, it would be wise to do your own investigation and consider where you might go if the government is not around to herd you like cattle into a place of their choice due to certain circumstances prevailing.

Paying rent or your mortgage may be impossible. As a result of so many homeowners losing their homes during the Depression from the entire nation literally being out of work, the government can now put a freeze on foreclosures and allow people to stay in their houses. However, also during the Depression, many renters were evicted for non-payment of rent. Whether or not you are allowed to stay in your apartment without paying rent will be determined by either the government or the building owner. If you are put out and if the phones are not working you cannot call "911" or the Fire Department or a taxi. You will have to go for self and find a place for yourself, or commandeer a place for yourself that is vacant. This is an issue which should be discussed with your entire family, extended family or close neighbors and friends to determine which options may be available to you. If you live on the 12th floor in an apartment building, or on the ground floor in house, it will be best if you barricade and bar your windows and doors as best you can. Form some kind of group committee to address these potential problems. Since we basically distrust each other this is going to be very difficult to do, but do it we must if we intend to survive. One family working alone will have a very hard time trying to make it. You need to have people around you who are on your side and willing to work as a team. It is also a good idea to contact your church, your minister, the deacon board and all the men in any religious or social organization you belong to. If you don't currently belong, join. You may have to "squat" in an abandoned house. At that time your major interest will be shelter, not decor. If you have relatives down-south or in the mid-west, it would be wise to pack-up now and move to where they are to get out of the city because the city will no doubt be a bloody battlefield of frustration, anger, robbery, rip-off and hysteria. The local stores you frequent in your neighborhood will be plucked clean of any and all food of any kind faster than you can say 'what happened?' Every speck of edible content will be gone. After a week or two, food delivery trucks, if there are any, will be hijacked on the highways long before they reach your community corner store or supermarket. The price of gas is already starting to go up and will become "liquid gold," and hard to get. It will systematically be rationed and even if you have a car, you will probably only be able to drive as far as a tank of gas will take you. Some will try this method of escaping the city at the last minute if the opening occurs. The idea that armed groups of scavengers will vacate the city and travel to the far suburbs or mountains or other isolated spots may not happen.

It will take a lot of inspiration to drive as far as a tank of gas will take you, walk on foot the rest of the way (probably in sneakers), traveling over hill and dale, looking for houses or families to rob. Plus, if a bunch of people get the same idea the highways will be jammed with traffic, breakdowns and wrecks from the panic. Additionally, anyone who has the scruples to get out of the city to avoid danger will no doubt be prepared to defend their turf (and food). Pray for snow. Of course there is also the possibility that the Feds will close down the highways, expressways and turnpikes in order to maintain some semblance of order and set boundaries. The main roads will be used strictly for the military. If you plan to escape the city try traveling on county roads. Get a map of your location and study the highway and road systems.

We must have a plan because white people do not want us invading their communities trying to steal their food and water and they are organizing their guns and ammunition just for this purpose. The time to try to get our own is right now while we still have a short chance of getting supplies on our own. There are people who are arming themselves with guns and rifles to keep you from stealing their survival goods. The people who don't prepare, both Black and white, will be the greatest threat to us all and roving bands of thugs (and ordinary family folks) will be out on the prowl looking for food. People will turn on each other and behave like savages to get what they need. This is to be expected. It is the normal course of human behavior in any societal breakdown such as war, famine, flood, earthquake, or riot when police are not around. The fallout due to the technological breakdown of the computer system which keeps America going falls into this category. This information is not intended to frighten you, but it is intended to inform you of the general hazards you can anticipate in the city, the urban world.

GATHER ALL YOUR LEGAL PAPERWORK _
Organize the following information for each person in your family: Birth Certificate
Shot records for children
Report Cards/Baptism Records
Marriage License
Deeds, titles, insurance
Credit cards, loans,
Mortgages, payment booklets
Tax returns, W-2's
Diplomas, certificates,
 Passports, driver's license
Wills, Medical Cards,

GET YOUR HOUSE IN ORDER -
If your house is crowded with a lot of useless furniture, get rid of it or rearrange it so that you have a lot of extra room for you and your family. You may get stuck in the house for extended periods of time, depending on what's going on outside, and everybody needs space to keep from getting on each other's nerves. This is called "cabin fever." Resist.

It is also wise to place an emergency suitcase near the door filled with basic necessities for your family, such as clothing, important papers, money, small snacks, and a first-aid kit; so that if you are forced to leave your apartment in a hurry you can grab it on your way out the door to keep from being left with nothing. We are a people who love to gamble and take risks, so many of us will not believe that the problem is as drastic as predicted. Some do not want to face this kind of reality, they do not want their life disrupted, they have so many expensive material things, or they have a good job and fancy car and just can't handle the threat that it could all come to an abrupt end - so they will procrastinate, disbelieve, shrug it off, laugh or decide that there's no point in doing anything. But don't get frightened into a state of no-action or become overwhelmed at the situation. This is no time to freeze up and sit around inactive waiting on the whole thing to blow over. If others don't believe, there is nothing you can do but continue to prepare yourself. And don't tell disbelievers what you are doing or how much food stock you have.

When things go wrong in America on a national scale affecting several cities; our government now has Homeland Security(to fight and stop terrorism), a title suggesting that if we live in the 'homeland' we will be secure. To follow up on this theory of securing the public welfare, they also have "The Patriot Act." They define this organization as allowing American law enforcement sweeping authority to monitor electronic communications with little or no oversight. They can use roving wiretaps, sneak and peek warrants and other provisions. They can do all of this without informing the citizen in question if they suspect that person of being a "domestic terrorist." They have complete access to our emails, Facebook info, Instagram's, Twitter accounts etc. This includes phone calls, faxes, medical, financial and other private transactions.

Including your immigration status. They have already gained notoriety for capturing criminals who break the law and then go on line showing the loot and bragging about what they did. We have been tricked into using Smart Phone as a confession booth and we report sometimes our personal minute by minute activities for the entire world to see. We show little concern about our posts becoming public information possibly tapped by employees of USA Patriot Act. We are addicted to the Iphone and cell phone capabilities.

Incidentally the Patriot Act is a law enacted by the U.S. government that was signed by President George

W. Bush on 10/26/2001. (Public Law Pub. L.107-56), in response to the 9/11 attacks. The acronym stands for 'Uniting and Strengthening America by Providing Appropriate Tools Required to Intercept and Obstruct Terrorism Act. They are independent of the Homeland Security agency but they all support each other.

They are also involved in the handling of local protests or uprisings by American citizens unhappy with the way justice is metered out unequally when charging Blacks and other minorities with legal infractions. And when a problem escalates to civil unrest/marching or rioting, we will be the first to be detained, arrested and accosted for any minor reason.

Now since this organization specializes in tracking actions and movements; it is better to pay for all your survival foods and products with cash whenever possible. When things get crazy we will have to live without these services which are all traceable:

Food Distribution	Hospitals
Electric, gas and water utilities	Thermostats
Telecommunications	Beepers
Transportation (subways, cars & airlines)	Cell Phones
Manufacturing control systems	Cable
Banking services & Stock Market	ATM's
National Defense operations	Lotteries
Security systems	Jail Cells
Nuclear Reactors and Weapons	Elevators
Gasoline dispersal	Access Cards
Business data processing	Pawn Shops

GETTING OUT....LEAVING FOR GOOD

Other Americans know or suspect that we are dissatisfied with our conditions of living here in America and they are quick to recommend: "If you don't like it here then go back to Africa!" It's understandable since we are always mouthing about Africa being the Motherland and our homeland, so it's not unreasonable for us to have a special place in our hearts for the African continent. One of the ways to pay homage to our "homeland" is to refer to ourselves as "African-Americans." Africans don't refer to us this way but this is what most of us call ourselves. In the past several years those of us who can afford to have established a dual citizenship between America and Africa and established residences there and taken their children and families to the "Motherland." The African continent is generally not presented to us in a good light. Ever since the white people came up with their fictional idea about Tarzan, they gave Africa a bad rep by implying that some white dude went to Africa and learned more about it than the inhabitants who have resided there for millions, maybe trillions of years. Christian television shows flaunt pictures of our ancestors starving, eating dirt, raggedy and doing bad. This suggests that we don't know how to feed ourselves unless the white missionaries show us the way and convert us to Christianity. The African continent is the richest piece of land on the earth. It has been proven that all life started there and it's an historical fact that all standards and practices of civilization started there created by original Black people. These genius ideas were not discovered in Europe; as most of us were taught in public schools. So we do have the right to go back if we so choose. Africa is made up of over 50 countries and is 3 times as large as the United States. There are innumerable languages, governments, cultural traits, community systems and regulations according to tribe. The African continent is not all victimized by famine, genocide, war or discontent. If you plan to go there to avoid the hell that's soon to take place here you have to do some major research. Escaping hell is hard.

You need to examine your situation, age, income, skills, and so forth because no country wants criminals, vagrants, savage or broke visitors. Choose the location you are interested in and proceed.

Start with www.state.gov and travel.state.gov. They have information about traveling and living in every country on the planet. They are all worth a look.

Also www.firstgov/Topics/Americans_Abroad.shtml and the World Factbook will educate you further. It's not impossible but takes a lot of preparation.

Needless to say the internet is filled with info on foreign countries – Canada is included. Bye.

CHAPTER 2
(Handling your stomach)

FOOD
(And what to eat)

Recall the biblical passage about Sodom and Gommorrah. LOT, (a Blackman), was unable to convince the citizens to leave the city after he told them it was to be destroyed, because the people didn't want to leave their fine homes, clothes and jewelry. Don't get caught up in that scenario. Choose your life over your fine living room or other trinkets. You need your closets, shelves, drawers and under-bed space to store food and water. It would be wise to buy some of that cheap metal shelving and assemble it inside your house. You may not know it but grocery stores only replenish their stock about two (2) or three (3) times a week and they sell out fast during any crisis such as an impending snow storm, heavy rains or extremely cold weather. It is customary in the "hood" for us to go to the store several times a day, while the national standard is about three(3) times per week. You may have already experienced the frustration of trying to shop for food the day of a predicted heavy snow storm. The store shelves are emptied in a few short hours and the first things they sell out of is milk, bread and water. Avoid the rush and crowd of panic shoppers trying to buy food at the last minute.

In other words don't wait until **300** million other Americans stampede the super markets searching for food and other necessities. The time to start storing and saving food is right now. This moment. Immediately after you finish reading this book.

Remember, when NOAH first starting building his Ark, the weather was dry and the sun was shining. It wasn't raining. No water was in sight. But NOAH (a Blackman) had been warned that a flood was coming so he commenced to making preparations, and told everybody else to do the same. They didn't.

So even if you can't get anyone you know or love to start stocking up on food - you must do it anyway. And do it quietly not telling all your friends and acquaintances what you are doing. Hide the food away out of sight in your house until there is simply no more space available to do so. Traditionally the same people who laugh at and mock you for making preparations for something they don't believe in, are the same ones who will come banging on your door when the storm strikes. Some people will feel that they don't need to prepare as long as they know someone who is. You become their contingency plan and they show up demanding you share.

START out by buying a few extra cans of food each time you go to the store. Buy the largest cans available in the foods you and your family like the most. But it will not be dinner as usual. So be realistic and no one will be overly disappointed. Rotate your stock and make sure expiration dates are 1-2 years away.
The rule, according to the U.S. Food and Drug Administration Center for Food Safety and

Nutrition is that Canned food packed in water or syrup lasts for 3 years, and canned food packed in oil last 5 years. Dehydrated (or freeze-dried) food in cans last 10 to 20 years. However, use it before then.

Take advantage of can-good sales and other dry-goods such as rice, beans and pasta. (Beans take a very long time to boil to cook, so don't end up with a lot of dry beans with nothing to cook them on.). You may have to re-package some of dry-goods to keep out roach or mice infestation. Do not use glass - it breaks, and do not use tin or metal because they rust and may contaminate your food. Use the largest plastic containers you can find, or large plastic garbage cans (leave the food inside the package they came in) and just stack them in the plastic garbage can and use wide clear cellophane tape around the lid to seal it. But before you seal it drop in a few bay-leaves because they keep out tiny bug infestation even if the dry-goods are still sealed in their original package, it is a good idea to throw in a few bay leaves for good measure. You want to keep all moisture away from your stored food. Do not store your food directly on the ground or on concrete floors because moisture will seep in and spoil it all. Keep it away from heat.

There also exists a product called "OXYGEN ABSORBERS" for food storage called ZPT 500 Oxy Absorbers. (or Nitrogen packs). You should put a few of these packets in your large food containers. Use one (1) per every 3 gallons of

stuff you store in the same container. There is also a product called "DESICCANT" a military spec silica gel canister, used to keep your valuables dry. (including food lockers). They keep the air and moisture out. Check Survival stores. These are very potent poisonous chemicals and must be discarded as soon as you open your storage barrels or pails. **DO NOT PUT THEM BACK INTO YOUR DRY-GOODS.**
Bad stuff can happen to your food if it is stored under improper conditions. It can suffer nutrient loss, spoilage by microorganisms, loss of color, flavor or aroma and texture. Inspect your stock frequently and try to rotate it often, eat some of the old and replace it with new items over the course of the year. Buy your food now while it is plentiful so you will not be in hysterical desperation about how you are going to feed your children or extended family.

Now this is an important chapter because we know how we like to eat – all the time. Storing food is a foreign idea to us.

Can goods, dry goods, and dehydrated foodstuffs are the best to store for long periods of time. They all have a shelf-life from 2 to 10 years. Please figure out how to buy the same foods or similar foods that your family currently eats, because if you start trying to feed them new foods or new tastes which they are not used to you will have mealtime rebellions which will distract you from your main mission of survival. Try out different menus on your family to get them accustomed to eating emergency foods. You may have to eat some canned foods right out of the can without cooking them if your gas or electric stove is not functional due to the computer collapse. A good BBQ grill is a good choice if you have a place to cook outside. Do not try to operate a BBQ grill inside. Some modern grills work with Propane tanks. Some of us will not have anything to cook on and we will have to eat straight out of the can. If you let rice or pasta sit in a small amount of plain water, they will soften up enough to eat. Explain the situation to your children and family so that they can get mentally prepared to cope with this. It will not be life as usual and you will not be able to run out to Kentucky Fried or Burger King to get a meal. Sometimes you can ask your grocery store owner or manager to order cases of food for you so you can get them at a wholesale or cheaper price. Often your local community center may know of a co-op which is when you chip in with several other people to buy basic food in bulk and split it down on the price. It could be referred to as collective buying. For instance, probably everyone you know eats rice, beans and pasta. So in actuality all of you could by a 50 pound bag of each once a month at a reduced price, instead of each of you individually purchasing several boxes of each per month at almost twice the price. Many cities also have low cost food suppliers such as Sam's Place or Jethro's or the like, and they not only have good bargains, but it's sometimes possible to talk to the manager and arrange to buy any cases of foods they no longer want to carry or do have left over. The only problem you have shopping at one of these places is that they keep a running list of ID on all their customers, and a list of the types of food they buy and the quantities. If the government enforces their rules about anti-hoarding, or limits the amount of food each family can purchase to 7 days, they may be able to verify your name and address and show up at your house demanding to confiscate your goods. So it is best to convince a store owner to order extra for you and buy it wholesale directly from him. But you definitely can get this food for a lower price if you shop in the right place and use the right technique. Reduce the variety of items in your diet. Stop eating so many varied foods. Select several and eat them over and over prepared in various ways. Learn to make do, if not, the shock of not being able to eat the same foods you're used to eating can drive you nuts.

HOUSE PLANTS -
While many of us are mini-horticulturists and enjoy having a house full of all sorts of plants, flowers, and exotic greenery, it's time to sit them outside of the house or give them away or uproot them and throw them out. If you are going to grow plants, now is the time to learn how to grow a few plants that you can eat instead of just admire. Plus, you will not have the extra water to feed to a plant that does not produce an edible leaf or root. There are several food plants which can be grown indoors, in apartments or in houses, basements or attics or windowsills, in the same flower pots you have been using. This

is called **APARTMENT VEGETABLE GARDENING** -
Read the directions on the seed packets, or start with mini-plants (seedlings) available from any garden store, and make sure that each plant will receive at least 5-6 hours of direct sunlight daily. You can grow these foods right inside your house:

        Tomatoes, carrots
        small fruits, peppers
        leaf lettuce, onions, leeks,
        radishes, beets, eggplant
        Herbs - parsley, basil, mint, chives

You can grow all of these plants in your own home and have enough produce to help feed your family. You will also enjoy the thrill of growing and eating your own food. Get a book on indoor gardening now. Start out with a few now and eat what you can.

Get used to spending less money on your current food bill so that you can spend it to buy food for the year 2000 famine. Yes, famine.

Start saving enough food to feed your family for at least three (3) months. You will be surprised at how much food this turns out to be. After you have saved enough for the three (3) months, start all over again and save enough for another three (3) months. Enough for a full year supply. If you break up the approximately six (6) months we have left before the year 2000, it makes it easier to tackle and simpler to accept. Each time you go to the store buy something extra for your stash. Get everyone in your family to do the same thing. You have got to stay conscious of this and keep it on your mind so you can have peace of mind later when many about you will be freaking out.

There are other spiritual and futuristic ideas coming out daily on the internet. The prophecies range from Jesus returning to earth and punishing the sinners to detailed information about the New World Order which includes descriptive passages from the psychic network. Certain Black people have ridiculously gone back to the horoscope readings and numerology. It seems we have run out of things to do or believe in. But there remains a global hope and expectation that the coming years will usher in a bright new era of high righteousness and world peace. In the meantime it is best to stock enough food to last us until this grand change occurs.

Right now there are many blood suckers of the poor who are plotting on how they can make money or become rich off of this situation when people will be in such dire straits that they will be willing to do any and everything to relieve their condition. Others will continue to capitalize on the demoralization, sickness and fright of our people. You do not want to be in that number. Prepare now.

The next type of food to try to get a hold of after you have a good quantity of canned goods, in the large, what they call #10 size cans (like restaurants use) of dehydrated foods sold in SURVIVAL food stores which have seemingly popped up all over. There are multiple choices such as:

    Powdered eggs, butter and cheese (you just mix with water)
    All types and flavors of soups
    Broccoli, peas, carrots, corn, onions
    Vegetable mixes, tomato sauce
    Peanut butter, spices
    Herbs, grains, honey, sprouts
    Powdered drinks, coffee, teas, milk
    Cereals, fruit flakes, granola
    crackers, grits, couscous
    Barley, oats, popcorn, crackers
    TVP (Textured Vegetable Protein)

TVP is a meat substitute flavored like beef, chicken, BBQ, taco or ground beef. It 's okay in small quantities and has a lot of salt in it. But it will break the monotony. TVP is made of soy flour. (not tofu). There are many tasty variations. These are for your food reserve. There is another type of survival food popular with the military called MRE's (Meals Ready to Eat), and they are delicious, come in a sealed packet which contains a full meal able to be heated or eaten straight out the pack. The one drawback on these tasty meals is that they are expensive, usually about $5.50 to $6.50/ea. per person per meal. That's abit too costly for us. They come in cases of 10 per.

All of the other foods listed above) rehydrate (fluff up to normal size) just by adding water, while some require some method of heating. (Explained in another chapter) They are delicious and cost about $12 to $35 per six #10

25

can, and each can contains, when reconstituted (mixed w/ water), about 20 to 50 servings. (Usually based on 1/2 to 1 cup per serving). They come with resealable lids. The prices my seem expensive initially but just remember that each can contains up to 50 servings. Please don't forget to get two (2) good MANUAL CAN OPENERS. This type of food has been around since the war and are usually just sold for camping or a act of God emergency such as flood, earthquake or tornado. The so-called "Militia/Survivalist" groups also purchase this type of food for their preparation for the eventual breakdown of American society and law enforcement or an impending race war. They reportedly have had food stored in trailers and bunkers for over twenty years. They are smart if they have. Now we must do the same thing except we are joining the fray very late in the game, and have very few resources to get everything we need. Some of these Militia groups host Gun Shows or Survival Shows periodically around the country. They are professional business people, family groups, and helpful vendors who have a lot of information, books and catalogs on survival and all related components. Look for the signs. They usually have their shows at convention centers, farmer's market or other meeting halls around town or just outside of town. Take the time to look for one of these shows in your area. They carry ALL sorts of items you will need - and wish you had. Hunger is a great motivator and can become all encompassing and prevent you from functioning and thinking normally. Get ready now.

VITAMINS - During times of extreme emotional duress your body need more nutrients to compensate for your loss of peace and reduce your stress. Start buying vitamins and minerals of all kinds(including children's multi-vitamins) and certain herbs for your family. Check your expirations dates to make sure they are good for at least 1-3 years or more. You can still use expired vitamins and herbs if need be as long as they do not look or smell spoiled. And don't get big capsules or pills that are hard to swallow. Get small sizes and chewable when possible. Get bags of raw leafy herbs to make tea with and also use as food They tend to last indefinitely if stored properly.

PETS - (dogs, cats, birds, fish)
While it is understandable that you love your pet, you must remember that pets cost money to feed and maintain. Of course a good watch dog may be a good investment, but dogs tend to eat a lot of food and have to be walked or let out and let back in, may get sick, may take up too much space, cause odors and get in the way. You may not have enough food to feed your dog and your family at the same time. It may be unthinkable at the moment, but you may have to let your dog go. Folks all over America may be forced to part with their pets because they can't feed them and cannot bear to watch them starve. This will create the additional problem of starving wild dogs roaming the streets day and night looking for food - and plowing into your garbage trash looking for scraps.

27

trash problem by freezing your garbage A cat serves only minimal purpose to catch mice or entertain. But cats shed hair, cause odors, get in heat, get sick and have to be let out. They also eat special food which you may not have or may run out of. Birds and fish only eat a small amount of pet food and if push comes to shove you can eat the bird and fry the fish. This sounds harsh but when food is short every edible source must be considered. There are some races of people in America who eat cats, rats and dogs - right now. So it is not out of the question. Horses are also a good source of meat for human consumption. Those pesky pigeons you see in the park, on the street, roof or parking lot may have to be your next meal. Pigeons eat trash sometimes but they are just another bird (fowl) in the final analysis and birds can be plucked, cut up, washed and cooked. This also goes for seagulls, blue birds, red birds, ducks, etc. There are also animals and fish in the Zoo or Aquarium which can be eaten in an emergency.

Now is the time to get your food, plants and vitamins stocked before the government issues laws against hoarding and limits the amount of food each person can buy.
       It seems that every country, at one time or another, uses FOOD to control the populace. Food is the best method of population and birth control ever discovered by our rulers. It is a relatively nonviolent way to reduce population numbers and get rid of the unwanted who perish mainly

because they are unprepared. Everywhere people are dependent upon outside agencies for their food, they are subject to being ruled by the suppliers at will. The last group we want to fall out with is the food suppliers because we are unable to provide food for ourselves. White people are not dependent upon us for their food, but we are totally dependent upon them for ours. We spend our time on food selection and preparation only. Think about it, the very staff of life; food, is out of our reach and can be taken from us, withheld or rationed by those in charge. There are many multifaceted plans currently being developed by the government to take over and manage the food supply.

Food will be used to rule, manipulate and control the people from coast to coast. We are all at risk.

*There is a reference list in the back of this book giving a few Survival Store locations to purchase emergency food and other survival products. Try to find the closest supplier to your location. You may even want to visit the store in person –or- just order conveniently on line. Shipping is really cheap for most of these products.

*We each eat about 5 ½ pounds of food a day @ 600 calories per pound totaling from 3,000 to 3,500 calories a day. Of course this is way too much but this is generally what we are accustomed to eating. 1000-2000 is more feasible and healthy.

Chapter 3
WATER
(How to get it, store it and purify it)

Normally healthy individuals can live for a little over 3 weeks without food, but we can only live without WATER for about 10 days. A human can survive on as little as 4 ounces of water a day if necessary.

We live in such a wasteful society. We throw away perfectly good food – and water- daily. Consumers (us) and businesses waste a tremendous amount of food compared to other countries.

Each person in your household will need at least one (1) gallon of water per day to be used for everything from drinking to personal hygiene. This is quite a bit less than the usual 50 gallons or so per day we are accustomed to using for showers and baths, flushing the toilet, washing hands, brushing teeth, drinking and cooking, and rinsing off various kitchen objects. You can add to this watering your houseplants, and filling the dog and cat dishes, doing the laundry or washing the dishes. We take running water for granted. Many of us don't even know where our local source of water comes from.

The first thing we need to be aware of is that water is very heavy and takes up a lot of space. A gallon jug of water weighs a whopping eight (8) pounds. If you can afford it, get into the habit of buying a gallon a day from now on until the end of the year. That would be over 200 gallons of water weighing about 1600 pounds. Another option is to store your water in those five (5) gallon plastic water jugs used for those portable rented water coolers. Sometimes you can purchase these from the supplying company.

But the most expedient way to store water in your home (our neighborhoods), is to just wash and clean out the 2 and 3 liter soda pop plastic bottles and fill them with regular tap water from your faucet. To treat the water so it will stay purified drop several drops of basic bleach (Clorox) into each bottle. Use a standard dropper such as the ones that come with herbal medicines or tinctures in it. You can purchase these at a drug store or wash and rinse one out that you already have. This is called the Basic Bleach Water Treatment Method (5.25% Sodium Hypochlorite). Don't worry about poisoning the water from using bleach. This is the scientific recommended method. If the water from your faucet is cloudy, just double the amount of bleach in each bottle.

BLEACH STERILIZATION FOR WATER:
1 Liter bottle   2 drops   1/2 Gallon   8 drops
2 Liter bottle   4 drops   1 Quart   2 drops
3 Liter bottle   6 drops   5 Gal jug   1/2 tsp.
1 Gallon jug   8 drops
* If your water is cloudy double the drop amounts.

If you have a basement, garage, enclosed porch or balcony, you can store as much water as you have space for. Keep it in a darkened place if possible and cover it with a tarp or heavy dark plastic if you have to store it outside your place.

When the crisis starts you will still have time to fill up your bathtub and save about 15 to 20 gallons more. If you have access to your hot water heater, turn it off, drain it and you can have another 40 to 75 gallons. The tank on the back of your toilet (clean water) will give you about 3 gallons more so clean it out and stop using those blue deodorizing tablets or any other fragrance pellet.
It maybe winter so rain and snow water can be collected in clean buckets. If you know how you can also siphon it someway and pour it into bottles.

DO NOT USE REGULAR MILK CARTONS TO STORE WATER IN - They are biodegradable and will burst or leak within a few months. And do not use metal containers unless they are made of stainless steel.

If you have a water bed it will hold a lot of water. Always remember to purify any water coming from an unusual source so as to destroy algae and any other microorganisms.

ODD WATER SOURCES OUTSIDE THE HOME:
Fire trucks   Pet Shops
              Fire hydrants
Indoor pools at hotels   Laundromats
(Boil or purify all sources)
Spas and restaurants also have available water. Schools and recreation centers that have pools, and ice companies all have some type of water in mass or frozen ice cubes. You will search everywhere if you run out of water.

There are three (3) common ways of purifying drinking water: 1) Boiling (2) Chemical Disinfectants such as chlorine, iodine or household bleach, and (3) Filtration through a ceramic or sand filter.

THE BEST METHOD OF STERILIZING WATER is to boil it for at least 10 minutes to kill bacteria and viruses. Iodine tablets called "water purification tablets" are available at sporting goods, outdoor camping, or mountain climbing stores. These tablets should not be used over a couple of weeks and only if you have nothing else. You may have access to other unique sources of water but please consider it all contaminated and use one of the above purification procedures to cleanse it.

If you live near a park pond or lake, you can collect water from there and use it to wash clothes - after adding bleach and detergent as usual. But your problem will be transporting it back to your location.

Buy a washboard and indoor clothes drying rack along with a large plastic or metal container for washing clothes. This project starts in winter so it will be very cold outside most of the time. If you are able to survive until spring consider yourself lucky.....blessed. Preserve your water.

Some people who have dirt in their back yard may try to drill a small well to get water from beneath the surface of the earth. Drilling a backyard well will cost about $2-3,000 but will be well worth the expense when the time comes. Call your City Hall and find out about zoning laws regarding digging a well. SAVE WATER. At all cost SAVE WATER. We cannot live without it.

It is also a good idea to purchase some of that water-less shampoo for washing hair. You just apply it to dry hair, allow it to penetrate, then comb and brush out. You will not have a lot of water to waste on long luxurious hair washing, perms or using hair color. Have a set of round plastic or metal basins to be used for washing/cleansing the body. Get a hard soap because it will last longer. Use 1/2 gal. of water. Stock up on lotions, skin softeners, deodorants and any other daily personal hygiene products you use. Do not worry about brand names or special fragrances, just get a large quantity of body products including toothpaste and mouthwash.

When it rains you can create some kind of funnel or cistern system to drain the water from your roof and roof pipes, or from your windowsill. Rain water is usually considered pure enough to drink or wash your hair in. One inch of rain falling on 50 square feet of surface makes about 25-30 gallons . If you are going to collect this from your roof keep in mind that one cubic foot of space holds about 7 gallons of water, and if you multiply that (7 gallons times 8 lbs per gallon), you are adding 56 extra pounds of weight per every cubic foot of water on your roof. It would actually be safer to put large containers on your roof to collect the rain water in. A child's plastic swimming pool, weighed down with rocks will work as well. You can easily pick out the debris. Or
you can purchase a Deluxe Portable Water Purification system for about $80 which is

certified to meet USEPA standards for purification against cysts and viruses without the use of pesticidal chemicals.

It will filter out sediment, silt, dirt, rust, algae and radioactive particles and other contaminants.

SANITATION AND HUMAN WASTE DISPOSAL:
No matter what you eat or drink, you and your whole family will still have to use the toilet. Once the water system is no longer functional and there is no system to remove human sewage you will need a new way to get rid of urine and bowel movement.. First you drain all the water out of the tank on the back of your toilet, the bowl will have a little water left in it. Clean it out with bleach or pinesol and put a empty (strong) plastic bag inside of the bowl. Fold the edges over the outside of the toilet bowl (tape them down with duct tape if possible), and allow your family to use the toilet several times before you lift the bag out, tie it off and find someplace to bury it underground. This system will also work with a sturdy bucket that you can also line with a strong plastic bag. If you use the bucket system, use two (2) buckets (pots) - one for urine and one for feces. A plastic 5 gallon bucket is a good choice. You can buy a toilet seat and lid to put on top of it. Have at least two (2) small shovels for this purpose. Nothing can create flies, maggots, rats or roaches faster than the improper disposal of human waste. Pre-select a spot near your house where there is a dirt lot or park. Bury your waste as deep as you can. You can dig a ample deep hole and put a couple of

boards across it so that you use it a few times before covering it back up with dirt. Cover it well. Stock several pair of heavy plastic gloves and disposable face masks. All it will take is a few uncaring nasty people to start using the bathroom on the street for the entire neighborhood to have rat and disease problems. Composting Toilets (a waterless solution) are convenient and require no plumbing. It is self-contained, uses no chemicals and is odor free. Compost and Chemical toilets are available in survival or camping stores. The latter has chemical salts which help break down the waste and reduce the odor. It is also possible to buy certain other chemical solutions to aid in the disposal of human excrement and reduce the smell. Stock ammonia and disinfectants for use with your sanitation system. Wear a mask.
TOILET PAPER IS A MUST! Start now and buy as much toilet paper as you can. Buy the cheapest you can find and store it in a dry place. Monitor how much each person uses because nothing is worse than running out of toilet paper. Since you will not be flushing anything down the toilet, you can also buy extra paper table napkins, soft paper towels and nose tissues. All of these can be used as toilet paper in an emergency. Toilet paper will be like money and you will be able to use it for barter and trade to get other things you may need. Toilet paper is a luxury.

CHAPTER 4
Cooking, heat and light replacement

At last count there are about 8,000 electrical power plants run by over 40-50 million embedded chip systems supporting 500,000 miles of high voltage power lines. Our electric companies do not always run independently. Many of them, located all over the country, have co-joined power grids with Nuclear Power Plants and they are co-dependent on each other. About 20% of the nations electric is generated from these interconnected Power and Nuclear plants. The Nuclear Regulatory Commission (NRC), say their plants monitor nuclear radiation and if they can't monitor reactor coolant levels and fuel handling systems, they will shut down and withdraw their support to the various electrical power companies around the country. Additionally, all nuclear weapon systems - in all nations, are computer dependent and are controlled by computers with date codes. Any hint of malfunction and the NRC is obligated by law to shut the entire plant down. They do not want to have a repeat of the devastating 1979 Three Mile Island meltdown when radioactive particles was accidentally released into the atmosphere and prompted the evacuation of thousands of Pennsylvania residents.

You can check the internet to get any updated or changes in the stats mentioned above. Most of us are accustomed to having power outages for a few hours to a couple of days due to technical problems, weather or outdated equipment.

We tend to handle these short lived inconveniences plus we rely on warm weather or extra blankets to see us through. What we're discussing here is an extra-long period of not having a regular heat source – possibly in winter. If you have a fireplace learn how to use it. Keep extra blankets and sleeping bags and extra gloves and socks. Buy a ton of those instant heat packs. They last a long time a can often be reused. Be careful of burns because these packs get really hot and last a few hours. Also keep some of this stuff in your trunk especially blankets and heat packs.

Keep a few large trash bags for making ponchos. Hard times are hard times and they level the playing field – into 2 categories, either a person is ready or not ready. History shows that we usually are not ready.

Having a regular flashlight is not enough but if that's all you got place it on a table in the center of the room with the light towards the ceiling and it'll light up the entire area until the batteries run out.

Living without electricity will be a real test for us because in this age of high technology we have all this equipment that has to be fed electricity.

> You may have food and you may have water, but you will also need, and want to have a way to cook or heat your food and stay warm. A good Kerosene heater is best if you can manage to store up enough kerosene. The first good thing about using Kerosene as a fuel is that it is NON-EXPLOSIVE. It costs less, burns longer than other fuels, stores for an indefinite period of

time, can be used for light, heat and cooking and can be bought for about **$3-$4** a gallon. It is inexpensive and safer to store. There are special "BLUE" plastic containers that say "Kerosene" imprinted on the sides especially made to transport Kerosene. They come in 2 1/2 up to 5 gallon containers. You can stay warm from a kerosene heater, cook on the top of it and it will provide minimal light. Unfortunately, the first four months of the year are generally cold and it will be very difficult to store enough Kerosene to last for at least four (4) months. If you live in a house with a fireplace all you have to do is build up a good wood supply. A wood-burning stove is even better. But a kerosene heater is a good solution for heat in a regular apartment. KEROSENE LAMPS are a good choice to provide a very bright light source and a little bit of warmth for hands. Those little red lanterns similar to the ones used by the railroad are cheap, only about $10 each, but they do smell like kerosene so they must be used in a well ventilated area. There are all sorts of other lamps which can be fueled with Kerosene or Lamp Oil. Lamp oil comes in pints, quarts and gallon quantities and costs from $1.99 to $4.99. They often have a floral scent which is good for aroma therapy to make you feel better. These lamps can cost from about $10.99 to $29.99 but they are attractive and a good investment, and can be carefully carried from room to room if necessary. They are available at Survival stores, department store lamp sections and places like K-Mart, Target and Walmart. You will have to learn to perform most

of your in-house tasks in front of a window to benefit from the daylight. Read, cook and sew during the day. Sleep, talk and make plans at night. Get your lamps before they are all gone.
Invest in a few good sleeping bags, military or domestic types, able to generate heat in temperatures down to 21 degrees or less. There are also double sized sleeping bags to fit 3 children or 2 adults. There are purse size "Mylar" blankets made of a foil like material designed to keep in body heat. They also make a good rain covering. About $3/ea.
There are "Hand and Body Warmer" packs that only require squeezing the packet to heat up, and they heat up and last for hours. They only cost about 50 cents or $1.00 a pack. It is a good idea to have a case of these on hand to keep hands and feet warm in the bed at night. Construction workers who work outdoors often use them in their gloves or boots to keep warm. They are odorless and non-toxic.
For those who have electronic or mechanical knowledge Gas Powered Generators are great. They can be plugged into a wall socket with a special connection and allow you to operate your refrigerator, washer and dryer, television (if there is any), and radio. They come in 300 to 5000 watts of available electrical power and if you use it sparsely, they can provide you with days of electrical power. Examples of how much power (wattage) is required for standard appliances are:

Microwave	500-1500 watts
Radio	30-100
Refrigerator/Freezer	600-2500
Television	100-350

Electric Skillet	1300
Washer	1150-2300
Light Bulbs	(as indicated on bulb)

Generators can be dangerous to maintain because they run off of gasoline only. DO NOT STORE GASOLINE IN THE HOUSE. Keep the generator outside because of the fumes. The required containers are "RED" and have the word 'gasoline' imprinted on the plastic carriers. Incidentally, Generators cost between $699 to about $1500 new. An industrial model providing 15,000 watts of power costs about $10,000/ Often used ones are available for less.

If you really want to be modern you can outfit your windows with SOLAR PANELS which provides electricity powered by the sun or bright day light. Solar Panels can be quite expensive costing about $99 per panel, and you will need several panels to cover each window. Solar panels are jet black colored panels to absorb the sun's heat. You can heat some water during the day by just running it through a Black pipe in the sun. You can cover any pipe with Black tape or paint some PVC pipe. Another grassroots option is to use a regular car battery hooked up to an inverter to generate power to run appliances or lamps. You will need some basic engineering knowledge to do this.

Battery powered flashlights are good for as long as they will last and if you use them sparingly and manage to keep the children from playing with them, they will serve you well. Especially if you have a solar powered battery charger. The last, and probably most popular form of alternative energy is a CANDLE. You can buy candles that will stay lit as long as 50 hours. They cost about $9/ea. A very inexpensive candle source ($1 to $2/ea.) are those tall prayer candles that come in various colors in a tall cylinder like jar. These candles have been tested to last for 7 days, lit all day, around the clock. They are cheap enough to buy by the case and are somewhat safe because the flame is always down inside the jar. They also provide a little hand heat and room heat if the doors are closed tight.

DO NOT USE those 12" long table candles because they do not have a stand, are too light weight, and have an exposed flame which can fall over and start a FIRE! Every lit flame you use for light MUST BE enclosed in glass or covered in some way to prevent the flame from touching other items and starting a fire. You need candles which will stay lit a long time, and these thin candles produce a lot of wax and burn too fast to be of any real benefit. Sterno cans of fuel can be used with a rack under aluminum pans to heat or cook food in. They are the same set-up you see at buffet tables used to keep the food warm. Sterno is relatively inexpensive and costs only about 1.00 a can. You will need several dozen if this is your choice for cooking. Everything you purchase from a Survival store will come with intensive instructions and directions to keep you from ruining your project or harming yourself. READ.

PROPANE canisters are another fairly safe choice to use for operating portable camp stoves. Propane comes in various sizes and can be refilled - if you have access to a propane tank somewhere for storage. They are bulky to store.

COMMUNICATIONS -
Smart Phone – CELL PHONES – TABLETS

It wasn't so long ago that everyone was excited about having a "beeper" to contact each other to send a short message or ask for a return call. Today technology has grown so fast especially in the area of cell phones. Some of them can cost almost a $1,000 depending on what types of services you want. We lose them, break the screens or drop them in the toilet but we replace them immediately because we believe we need them to survive. But if there are power outages, hurricanes, earthquakes, economic disruptions, job loses, epidemics, blizzards or food shortage crises; we are at the bottom of the ladder and we bet believe that nobody is going to look out for us.

Telecommunications could go down - this means that the telephones will not work and you will not have your normal means of communication. Telephones, to us, are essential, but since the telephones will not be functional, you will need an alternate method of communication so you can stay in touch with some of the rest of the world and not feel so isolated, and know what's going on around you and across the nation. Your choices are:
    Walkie Talkies
    CB Radios
    Hand-held Short Wave Radios

These and other communication systems are available at hardware or camping stores. None of our communication systems are independent – some need batteries only but your 'Smartphone' will have to be charged to send a text or receive emails. Of course while it's unlikely that all of these systems will go down at the same time remember that during any disaster cell phone towers get overloaded. Of course those of us who still have the now old-fashioned "land line" will be able to communicate for a longer time. Another instrument which is a bit independent is a solar operated radio with a hand-crank. You'll need a radio anyway to keep abreast of any announcements that may affect your neighborhood.

Drills are periodically done by the military to examine the entrances and exits to urban areas, monitor behavior in highly populated zones and make provisions to control certain vicinities in a civil disorder emergency. Plans were made during the 60's riots and updated in 1992 after the Rodney King uprising in Los Angeles. In recent history we have seen the military/National Guard in action to control protesters in several cities where citizens were reacting to the seemingly random shooting/murder of African-American men and women across the country. The police now have modern weaponry purchased from the government left over from some of their wars. Big tanks and guns were seen on the streets of our cities mimicking a war zone overseas.

This is not the kind of emergency planning we want to look forward to. The so-called law keepers showed the rest of us that Black Lives didn't matter and neither did any other kind that were in disagreement with their orders. It's safer to remain at home if at all possible. Check with your town and State government regarding local resources for emergency situations. Always go to the Red Cross site.

Whether it's an act of God or an intentional act by people, anarchy or any other kind of civil unrest; we have to be ready – if we want to live.

EXAMPLE OF A FIRST AID KIT:
Band-Aids
Sterile Dressings/pads
Gauze rolls
Antibacterial hand wipes
Latex gloves
Adhesive Tape
Antibacterial ointment
Cold Packs
Scissors
Tweezers
Face Masks
Pencil/paper
Whistle

You can add on any other items you choose. Keep this sack/backpack in a special area to be handy when you need it.

ALL ABOUT THE 'BENJAMIN'S'...

Banks (including ATM/MAC) machines all use computers to keep up with money and trade transactions. What if the Banks go down too, which is almost a surety if the electric power goes off? Right now 40% of Americans play the Wall Street stock market and Blacks are more involved in investing their money in Stock, Mutual Funds, etc., than at any other time in our history. We also hold more jobs in that category than ever before. Computers have paved the way for both of these activities to take place. Others of us spend a lot of time maxing out our credit cards. We use our debit card from the bank sometimes almost daily. Then there are those security deposit credit cards which require a cash deposit to get a credit card that says either Master-Card or VISA. We are allowed to use the card as if it were a real one - until our security deposit runs out. All of these transactions are run by computers which are interconnected all over the world so that we can use our credit cards nationally and internationally if we so choose.

We (Americas) spends over $119 Billion a year gambling. We have Casinos in 39 states, and Lotteries in 45. Blacks spend a lot of money daily playing the lottery and other games of chance. Some of us believe that hitting the lottery is the only sure way we will ever become rich. There is a constant cash-flow of some kind in our communities daily. Little do most of us know that our banks process transactions every few minutes in this new age of Cyberspace Money. Only 3% of American money is in circulation, the other 97% is done on computer screens. Money transfers are nearly instantaneous. While we may think that America has all the money and technology, 7 of the world's 10 largest banks are located in Tokyo, Japan - not here. While Wall Street and big banking conglomerates are not considered in our usual spending cycles, what happens to them affects our wallets directly. When the banks go off line and are unable to process transactions, make transfers, cash checks or conduct any other financial business the entire country will financially default.

It's a good idea to start saving any money you can. We, traditionally, do not have a good track record for saving money. We insist on instant gratification and as soon as we get any money, we already have a plan about what to spend it on. A saving plan for us has to be tailored to our lifestyles. We will have to try saving in small increments. Like saving small change, (not pennies). And for once, small change may be your best bet. Silver coins, especially those minted prior to 1965, are about 90% real silver. They are referred to as "Junk Silver." They will be a good tool to use to make purchases. Of course if you have Gold coins, you will be able to get just about anything you want. But gold in any form is currency. There is no gold-backed currency in the world. All currency is backed by debt and public faith.

Just as during the Depression of the 1930's, there will be people organized to do business deals of all kinds, attempting to capitalize on the desperation of others. During the Depression era people would gladly trade their solid Gold watches and diamond rings for a loaf of bread or even an apple when things got really tough and their cash money was no good and they were hungry. People also sold their real estate properties for little or nothing. It was during that time that many white businessmen got their financial start and garnered large blocks of properties obtained for outrageously low prices. Blacks had just come up out of slavery for about 75 years and our families were in the most desperate situation of all - especially in the North where they did not have access to land (dirt) to grow food to feed themselves. They lived in the city (Urban) areas just like most of us do now. Expect this to happen again on a variety of levels. The vultures are waiting.

We tend to like having cash money in our possession and show it off at every opportunity. This will be a good time to have a big stack of money – all in small denominations such as $5's and $10's, nothing larger than a $20 bill. Paper money is no longer backed by silver or gold but while it remains the only method of exchange we have, it will be better to have some $$$. Barter/Exchange will become popular – again. We may have to exchange money or goods for something else we need. Any cash money we have in the bank should be taken out ASAP because they may decide to close. That includes emptying your safe-deposit box.

Passing out a lot of paper money, even though it may be worthless, will make the public feel better for a while until they find that it is unacceptable for trade, and the people who have what they need won't accept it. Or that once they spend it they can't go back to the bank to get any more because the ATM machine's are out of service. Blacks already are a bit suspicious of banks. We distrust any system that locks our money up away from us. We like to touch our money - and see it. We feel even better if we can carry it around and flash it every once in a while. So even after the dollar fails, many of us will still be attracted to the idea of actually having in our possession a lot of paper money in large denominations. It will be very heartbreaking for many people in this country to witness the American dollar fall from grace at home and around the world. It has been said, by those claiming to know, that the FDIC backed up by the Government, will start to limit the amount of cash a bank customer can withdraw from the bank at one time. So it is best to start to rearrange your finances now before the real bank rush begins. That CD you have buried in your bank for retirement may change from being a Certificate of Deposit to Cash Dissolved - gone! Make your move now. All financial institutions will be affected - including the IRS and your Credit Union. Your Social Security Check, Child Support, Annuity, welfare allotment and any other form of electronic transmittal of money into your account - including any checks written on paper. Initially businesses, banks, phone companies, hotels, airlines, trains, buses, etc. will try to continue to function by applying their contingency plans. Currently major cities such as Flint Michigan and Philadelphia are suffering from lead contaminated water. Flint was the first to reveal they had an ongoing problem with bad water. That was a few years ago. Their discovery prompted other cities to evaluate their own water and to date 33 major cities report that they too have lead contamination in their drinking water. Nothing has been done except telling the citizens to test their own water, drink and cook with only bottled water and to be patient.

     A contingency plan is a "Plan B;" a plan to be put into action when your usual system won't work for whatever reason. These instructions are our "Plan B." We are so dependent we have never planned for or considered having a "Plan B" for survival. We have grown tolerant, unconcerned.

The white people who laid the plans for this country and it's various departments of operation to run a nation, are not going to throw in the towel easily. Their greed motivated by their desire to rule, has not been lost on their descendants (the white people who rule the country today), and their grand-sons and great grand-sons and great-great-grand-sons are going to do everything in their power to keep their control in tact, meaning white-owned and operated. They will not give up their holdings easily. Psychologically, they will not be able to handle it so they will be working hard to keep things functional on some level. Not necessarily to provide services or assistance to us, but to keep their massive egos in check. Historically they do not accept failure or defeat well. While we may measure our success based on how many material goods we own, they measure theirs by how many material goods they can produce and sell for a profit. Just like we are consumers now, most of us will be consumers during any collapse in our formal and informal structure that keeps America functioning. Right now popular TV shows and movies are featuring some re-invented characters called "Zombies." The behavior of Zombies shows them looking wild, savage, uncontrollable, ragged, hungry and ruthless in their quest to kill and eat the people who are not Zombies. They travel from neighborhood to neighborhood and come out mostly at night to rampage and pillage any area they can find where the residents have sustenance. They are brutal in their assaults and will eat the face and body of anyone they capture. This is how the apocalypse is being advertised. At some point there will be literally thousands of savages roaming around nationwide who did not prepare for the breakdown in society so they will be murderously desperate – crazy to find and destroy anything that they don't have.

Plus over the past few years many of the mental health care facilities and homes have been defunded and shut down. The occupants have been turned out into the streets destined to become homeless vagrants, beggars, disruptive personalities against an unwarned public and angry – mad at the society they believe has failed them. They will feel the same disappointment that sane people experience when fired, laid off or who are qualified but cannot find work. These days it does not take very much for a stressful situation with no remedy in sight to produce a Zombie personality.

The onslaught of the heroin epidemic which replaced crack, further adds to the discomfort of the working-class who are already struggling to make it. Adding to the heavy drug problem (those using hard drugs) is another class taking pills/prescription medications, all at the same time. Topping it all off is over the past few years nearly 30 states have approved legal marijuana/weed/pot, for medicinal and recreational use. It seems that nearly the whole country is on some kind of drug – legal or illegal. Predictably the people who smoke weed will commence to grow their own in the secrecy of their private locations. Pot, unlike heroin or crack; calms the smoker down, makes them nonviolent and woozy. They represent no real danger to the public. Alcoholics, on the other hand, will suffer if they don't have access to beer, wine or liquor daily if they are addicted to being drunk. All of these scenarios represent a problem if our way of life hits the fan and splatters negatively affecting us all.

Moving out of the city out to places like the mid-west is beginning to sound better and better since city, suburb and urban areas will be cluttered with random Zombies looking for drugs, food and water.

This book is to help you and your family (tribe) be ready to handle a disaster that lasts for about a week or so. It is up to each family to decide how much of a safety-net they want to have. Stocking up for 2-3 weeks is best. Of course, this may be impossible due to storage space limitations. Be aware that if you run out of food and your children are crying from hunger; you are a potential problem for the rest of us because the situation will possibly force you to hit the streets to try to take food from someone else so you can feed your family. Don't get caught in that position. Fuel for your car will also be a problem. Gas prices will go up and up and no amount of money will buy you more than the government allotted amount. Gas coupons may be issued. Kerosene, oil and diesel fuels will also become scarce. People will make runs on the banks to withdraw their money thinking that money will solve their problems. It won't. Not entirely.

Once the banks are unable to process accounts or cash checks, and people are not able to work because the computers are not operating; we may get reduced to a cash-less society. A cash-less society is when no money, or very little money changes hands for goods or services. Gold and silver will still be considered "real" money here and abroad. Now is the time for you to gather up all your gold and silver jewelry. That's your 10kt, 18kt and 24kt earrings, watches, rings and bracelets, they will take on a new value and you can use them as cash. The bulk of us will not have any gold or silver coins.

Bartering is always the system of trading and receiving goods and services during an extended crisis of any kind. There are always certain items which make the best mediums of exchange. They are:
>cigarettes, cigars, tobacco
>coffee, sugar,
>toilet paper, matches
>candles, lighters
>Wine, whiskey, beer

You will need some of these items for trade. You will not be able to hold a Yard Sale or Flea Market to sell your knickknacks to get money. Dispose of those types of items now before you get stuck with a lot of useless stuff with no value that just takes up space.

CHAPTER 5
Health, Medications and Mental Preparation

With the regular public systems disrupted resulting from
helpful places such as hospitals, emergency rooms and clinics will also be affected. This means you need to know something about applying first-aid, administering CPR, and treating medical problems with limited medications and resources. The American Red Cross offers basic First Aid training courses and CPR. Purchase a few medical books for home use and READ them. If someone in your family is Insulin dependent, now is the time to either

stock up on a several month supply of this medication, or to wean them off the Insulin in an appropriate way. ALL illnesses can be somewhat controlled and treated with diet. Now is the time to study up on techniques to eliminate pharmaceutical medications. Equipment and supplies such as catheters, ostomy bags, antibiotics, and any other medications or items considered "Maintenance Medicines," should be stocked up on now if you are able to do so. Gather the basics such as aspirin, bandages, salves, rubbing alcohol, pain relievers, allergy medications, cough syrup, children's medicines, cold remedies and peroxide. Include Tampax, Pads and disposable Douche kits. The following is a created distributed by The Honorable Elijah Muhammad to his followers over 75 years ago.

The Muslim Survival Kit
(Use this for your check-off list)

Thermometer (oral and rectal)

Aspirin	Sanitary Napkins
Alcohol	Hexol or Lysol
Adhesive Tape	* Charcoal
Gauze	Can Heat
Band-Aids	Sterno Stove
Epsom Salt	Coleman Stove
Baking Soda	Habaki Stove
Burn Ointment	Kerosene Lamp
Hot Water Bottle	Candles
Ice Cap	Matches
Sulfur (powder or salve)	Transistor Radio
Spirit of peppermint	Flashlight
Milk of Magnesia	Wool Blankets
Maalox	Sheets (bandages)
Keaopectate (for diarrhea)	Newspapers

Cotton   Ax and Shovel
Scissors
First Aid Book
                    * Pulverize Charcoal, take
2 layers of cotton, put charcoal between them,
dampen and use this as Gas Mask.

Antiseptic Solution   Table Salt
Sodium Chloride Tabs.   Sodium Citrate
Triangular Bandage   Bath Towels
Drinking Cups   Eye drops
Safety pins   Razor Blades
Toilet Soap   Splints
Tongue Blades   Measuring Spoons
Water Purification Tablets   Vaseline

This day has been expected for a long time and these are The Messenger's recommendations to us to preserve our lives during times of duress.

PROPER CLOTHING -
This may sound a little strange but Men and women should own a pair of leotards/tights/leggings because they hold in heat. All clothes should be comfortable and thick, and you should be able to wear them for several days if necessary. If water is scarce, it will be anti-survival to use a lot of water to wash a lot of clothes several times a week. Build a supply of "throw-away" clothes so that if you have to discard them after they are dirty, you will not feel so badly about doing so. Stock up on warm socks, undershirts, long underwear, sweat suits, gloves, knit hats and plenty of underwear. Get most of this stuff in cotton fabric if at all possible. You may have to

sleep in your clothes to keep warm. If you are cold all of the time it will affect your mood and ability to function.

Make sure you have extra sets of eye glasses and contact lens, and plenty of condoms and birthcontrol if you use any. Remember, if the hospitals and drug stores are not in operation, you will not be able to go to the hospital to have a baby or get treatment for any venereal disease. Some hospitals have emergency generators which will work for a few days maybe, but patients in ICU and CCU, with severe ailments will not have permanent access to monitors and other sophisticated medical equipment run by electricity. Be prepared, study a good book on emergency medical care, natural childbirth at home, and setting broken bones or pulling teeth. Just because there is a national food, water and money crisis going on, life will proceed at its natural pace regarding human needs and people will continue to get sick, need emergency care and have life threatening ailments. During this time we will regret that we never did build any hospitals or First Aid stations of our own. We will think about all the social community centers and churches we built, and wish that we had used some of that money and expertise to build a medical center staffed by qualified non-white technicians. As of the printing of this book, we do not know how long this crisis will last, or what type of world we will have after the fall and destruction of this one. None of us in the inner-city can prepare for over a year due to lack of space.

MENTAL STATUS -
The biggest problem we'll have that will interfere with our emotional condition is FEAR. Fear of helplessness and unsurety. Study yourself, and think about how you really handle stress, fear, anxiety, pain, sickness, cold and heat, hunger and fatigue, boredom and isolation. Specialist say that the real danger to personal survival is the "desire for comfort." No one likes to be uncomfortable and this feeling can drive one over the edge if not monitored. This is no time to give in to the self-aggrandizement of having what is commonly called "a nervous breakdown." You must keep your wits about you and become stubborn, determined to survive. If you lose your lack of will you, and your loved ones, will be in serious internal trouble and the entire house will suffer from your mental weakness. Your personality plays the most important role in survival.

According to 1970 Department of the Army's Survival textbook, an army field manual, #FM21-76, the personal qualities you need to survive are:

a) Being able to make up your mind
b) Being able to improvise
c) Being able to live with yourself
d) Able to adapt to the situation
e) Remaining cool, calm and collected
f) Hoping for the best, preparing for the worst
g) Having patience
h) Being prepared to meet the worst that can happen.
I) Being able to "figure out" other people

j) Understanding where your special fears and worries come from, and knowing what to do, to control them.

This list is a good basic example of how to get control of your emotions and think this thing out before it arrives. Talk about it with your mate or family, rehearse emergency procedures and practice until you are programmed to take automatic action. Conquering fear of the unknown is our greatest obstacle. Fear is merely a lack of understanding of a situation and a lack of knowledge of what to do about it. This book is designed to provide solutions to help you remove the fear in each category of survival. Fear takes too much energy.

TRAINING FOR CHILDREN:
Keeping our children occupied and under control during any absence of essential services is paramount. Fortunately children are durable and can accept and understand more than we give them credit for. They must be toughened up to handle the chaos which is sure to follow the breakdown of the computer systems in America. We should calmly explain to them, using understandable terms and examples, exactly what will probably happen and what they must do to help. Give them definite duties, assign certain tasks to them, let them help with the shopping for the foods for your emergency pantry. Talk to them about a reduction in the use of water and about the possibility that they will be cold and have to eat different food. We do not want them surprised or traumatized by a power failure, closed businesses, coldness in the house, restricted outdoor play, school closings, etc. We must teach them about this in a way that makes it an adventure. Children love adventures - especially those that involve the whole family. Start stocking up now with board and card games, story books, lots of paper and crayons, coloring books, craft projects, jump ropes, balls, diaries, puzzles, etc. The children may be restricted in their outdoor time and therefore will need something to do inside the house to amuse and entertain themselves. Do not stock up on a lot of battery-operated hand-held video games - unless you have a solar battery charger. Living with no TV will be a real challenge to our children since we have allowed most of them to be raised and entertained

several hours a day by this instrument. They may go through a sort of withdrawal. They are used to looking at moving pictures with loud sound. Get a good radio (battery or solar powered) so that listening to the radio becomes a family activity. Assign a different person to listen to the radio at different times so you do not miss any important announcements. Somebody will be on the air giving out instructions, news and pertinent information about the status of your area - and the country. Make listening to the radio a serious responsibility - because it will be. Also teach your children to keep quiet about your preparations. Make it a confidential family matter. By doing this it will allow your children to notice what is going on around them.

Education will have to continue using home-school techniques. Start collecting school books, tablets, notebook paper and pencils. Work out a curriculum to follow to make sure your children continue to get some educational input albeit informal. Someone in your community may set up a school of some sort to service the needs of the displaced children.

Blacks are the highest populations in several major cities located in these areas. The current welfare cutbacks will add to the human chaos. Ethnic groups of teens, youngsters and babies will be a risk. It is already expected that when some marginal families are removed from the welfare and/or food-stamp rolls, the parents (mother or caregiver) may become so

61

despesperate that they abandon their children. With no regular allotment to count on to house or feed them, may children will be cast out to fend for themselves. Mothers/parents who are already on drugs and neglecting their children will use this situation to leave them. Many will be rounded up and placed into some of these detainment centers separated by age and sex. Youth gangs will be the most difficult to contain because they are street urchins used to living on the edge and rejecting adult authority. Expect roving gangs to rebel and plunder the inner cities searching for food and water. Plus, many of them have weapons and no conscience. Each family will have to make their own decision based on their own personal values about whether or not to try to take any of these children in to feed and care for them. Our elderly will be in the same position, unable to get out and get food for themselves, they will be found roaming the streets at the mercy of whomever they encounter. Many of them are medication dependent and being old and considered useless, it is unclear as to what will happen to them. They will not be of much service to a detainment center labor camp. Presently we have no independent system of services set up to care for poor non-white elderly. Meals-on-Wheels, the Red Cross and other community services for senior citizens will not be able to operate indefinitely without food deliveries, gas or electric to prepare food, vehicles to deliver food or shortage of aides to assist them.

IMPORTANCE OF RELIGION:

The importance of religion, believing in a higher power, a supreme being, will be of paramount importance during hard times. Whether we think its doomsday or the ushering in of the New World Order or the judgement between good and evil; will not matter when this event takes place. Albeit prayer and a religious belief system will be crucial, it is more important to be ready on a physical level and have everything in place you'll need to survive and defend your nest. It is a good thing to rely on the support/blessings of whatever God you believe in – because you *will* be calling on Him. Certain prophecies predict a massive race way, a war between the Europeans themselves and the Government or that the Creator Himself will show up. Whatever. Also the white Militia has been planning for a breakdown of society for over 40 years or so. They are busy training their wives and children to defend themselves and use weapon force if necessary.

While the government and corporate America will be working day and night to restore America to what it once was, there will be others who will seize upon this opportunity to dismantle the government as it stands, and replace it with a new idea of their choosing. Prayer will be the main line of defense for everyone. There will be crying, confessing of faults, shouting, purging and praying of every kind we know plus some new kinds we have never witnessed before. Everyone will be trying to get in touch with the God they believe in - hoping that He is the one who will come and save them. Churches, Temples and Synagogues of all denominations will fling open their doors to the masses seeking help and salvation. Be sure to have your own Holy Book in your home. You will turn to it seeking comfort and guidance during this upheaval. Every pot will stand on its own legs, meaning each individual will go through their own religious experience either bringing him or her closer to God, or complete disbelief in anything holy. This may be the greatest test of belief we have ever experienced. Work out a plan to defend your food, property and family. You may need it.

SECURITY and SELF DEFENSE
There is a criminal element inside and outside of urban areas who will try to take advantage of the absence of "911" rapid response from police. While the Constitution allegedly guarantees the right of every citizen to own and "bear arms," this is an individual decision based upon your own self-defense philosophy. Guns historically have harmed us more than they have helped us. Shootings committed in domestic situations remain at an all time high. And families who are forced to live in the same quarters indoors for an extended period of time may get on each other's nerves to the point of violence. There will be all kinds of disagreements about what to do and how to do it. Anyone in the house having a gun can become dangerous and put everyone at risk. As much as we would not like to think about it,

We will all need a-------

security system in place. If the electrical system goes down and the Nuclear Power plants are forced to shut down, there are laws on the book that demand that the police "911" system shuts off too. Think about it, if there are no street lights at night, no burglary alarm systems to go off, and no police to call; the stage will be set for looters and robbers to take to the streets scavenging, stealing and terrorizing businesses and people. Getting ready for this type of situation calls for us to get rid of "civilian thinking," and prepare for more of a "guerrilla warfare," climate. The streets could very well turn into a "Wild West" scenario, including wounded or dead bodies lying openly in the streets with no ambulance or mortician service to remove them. Adding to all of this hell will be DRUGS - people selling drugs and people starting on drugs, and people trying to feed their habit. This will go on until the local drugs run out, and with no way to get a new supply to replenish the market, things will get crazy between the drug dealers and their clients (users). Crime will soar.

MORE ABOUT LIQUIDS...

Regardless to what you have heard...DO NOT drink your own urine (nor bathe in it), because it contains salts and other waste products harmful to your body. Your urine is 95% water and 5% waste such as urea and uric acid and salts. Boiling will not purify urine. Our urine is harmful as a beverage. DO not drink it. Next, do not drink blood. If you drink blood you are ingesting the same filth and salt as in urine. It forces whatever water you have in your body to expel it.

EMERGENCY FOOD SUPPLIERS

wisefoodstorage.com
888-852-3879
    mypatriotsupply.com
    866-229-0927
beprepared.com
(emergency essentials)
800-999-1863
    thereadystore.com
    800-773-5331
Nitropak.com
800-866-4876

PRISONS and JAILS:
Statistics claim that there are 8 million people in jail worldwide with 25% of them located here in America - the only country claiming to be the "Land of the Free." These 2 million prisoners, men, women, teenagers and children, are housed in prisons all over the country. They each cost taxpayers about $40,000 a year per prisoner, to feed and maintain. The majority of these prisons are modern and updated to have their cell doors run automatically by computer.

People who we believe have broke the

law are not important to most of us.

This creates a problem for the nearly 1 million Black and other non-white people who are locked up. You can be sure that if there is a food shortage, the last people on earth to receive concern or consideration will be those who are in prison. If this group gets out, they will go seeking their families and friends, and those who are sane will become a real help to their communities. But those who are insane, will add to the problems on the street. Hopefully, the people of color who are in prison will hear this message and begin to prepare themselves for possibly sudden release or inhumane treatment from frustrated prison administrators.

Chapter 6
GOVERNMENT PLANS FOR THE UNREADY:

The entire American system for administering aid to the needy is based on a battlefield or disaster medical term called "Triage." This comes from a French word which means "to sort." It is traditionally used for sorting injured people into groups based on their need for immediate treatment. This term will apply when it comes to allocating food, water, and protection. Help will be given where it is perceived to be able to do the greatest good. While some will be in a pitiful condition they may not qualify for help from the government. This term "Triage" is based on the concept that you cannot attend to everyone so you must assist those with the best chance of survival. Triage is broken into three (3) categories:

1) Pass over those who can survive with no attention.
2) Ignore those who are too far gone to survive.
3) Assist those who have the best chance of survival

This is a system akin to natural selection, only the strong survive, separating the wheat from the corn.

Governments loves for their citizens to have a crisis, it gives them the opportunity to write new laws, create programs, increase taxes, spend money, and impose regulations - all under law. The American government is no exception, there are already procedures and laws in place to handle situations like Y2K is sure to produce. Poised for action.

THE KING ALFRED PLAN: (for Civil Disorder)
This is an alledged fictional description of what the government is capable of doing based on their secret plans. It is taken from the 1967 book titled:"The Man Who Cried I Am," by John A. Williams, a talented writer and researcher. This passage is used by his permission. (This account is similar to a follow-up of the Willie Lynch letter):

KING ALFRED PLAN

In the event of widespread and continuing and coordinated racial disturbances in the United States, KING ALFRED, at the descretion of the President is to be put into action immediately.

Participating Federal Agencies
National Security Council   Dept. of Justice

*849-899(?) King England, directed translation from the Latin Anglo-Saxon Chron.
Central Intelligence Agency   Dept. of Defense
Federal Bureau of Investigation   Dept. of Interior

        Participating State Agencies
        (Under Federal Jurisdiction)
National Guard Units   State Police

        Participating Local Agencies
        (Under Federal Jurisdiction)
City Police   County Police

Even before 1954 when the Supreme Court of the United States of America declared unconstitutional separate educational and recreational facilities, racial unrest and discord had become very nearly a part of the American way of life. But that way of life was repugnant to most Americans. Since 1954, however, that unrest and discord have broken out into widespread violence which increasingly have placed the peace and stability of the nation in dire jeopardy. This violence has resulted in loss of life, limb and property, and has cost the taxpayers of this nation billions of dollars. And the end is not yet in sight. This same violence has raised the tremendously grave question as to whether the races can ever live in peace with each other. Each passing month has brought new intelligence that, despite laws passed to alleviate the condition of the Minority, the Minority still is not satisfied. Demonstrations and rioting have become a part of the familiar scene. Troops have been called out in city after city across the land, and our image as a world leader severely damaged. Our enemies press closer, seeking the advantage, possibly at a time during one of these outbreaks of violence. The Minority has adopted an almost military posture to gain its objectives, which are not clear to most Americans. It is expected therefore, that, when those objectives are denied the Minority, racial war must be considered inevitable. When that Emergency comes, we must expect the total involvement of all 22 million members of the Minority, men, women and children, for once this project is launched, its goal is to terminate, once and for all, the Minority threat to the whole of American society, and, indeed, to the Free World.

Chairman, National Security Council
Preliminary Memo: Department of Interior

Under KING ALFRED, the nation has been divided into 10 regions (see accompanying map)

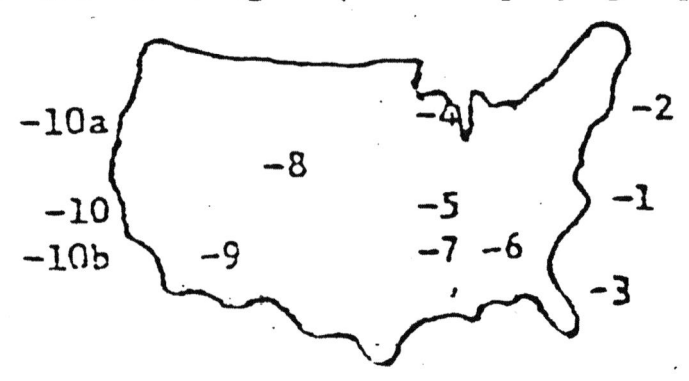

-10a
-10
-10b
-9
-8
-4
-5
-7 -6
-2
-1
-3

In case of Emergency, Minority members will be evacuated from the cities by federalized national guard units, local and state police, and, if necessary, by units of the Regular Armed Forces, using public and military transportation, detained in nearby military installations until further course of action has been decided.:

1 - Capital Region
2 - Northeast Region
3 - Southeast Region
4 - Great Lakes Region
5 - South Central Region
6 - Deep South Region
7 - Deep South Region II
8 - Great Plains, Rocky Mt. Region
9 - Southwest Region
10, a,b - West Coast Region

No attempt will be made to seal off the Canadian and Mexican borders.

Combined Memo: Security, Department of Interior
Department of Justice
Federal Bureau of Investigation
Central Intelligence Agency

There are 12 major Minority organizations and all are familiar with the 22 million. Dossiers have been compiled on the leaders of the organizations, and can be studied in

71

Washington. The material contained in many of the dossiers, and our threat to reveal that material, has considerably held in check the activities of some of their leaders. Leaders who do not have such usable material in their dossiers have been approached to take Government posts, mostly as ambassadors and primarily in African countries. The promise of these positions also has materially contributed to the temporary slow-down of Minority activities. However, we do not expect these slow-downs to be of long duration, because there are always new and dissident elements to replace the old leaders. All organizations of theirs are under constant, 24-hour surveillance. The organizations are:

1) The Black Muslims
2) Student Nonviolent Coord. Com. (SNCC)
3) Congress of Racial Equality
4) Uhuru Movement
5) Group on Advanced Leadership (GOAL)
6) Freedom Now Party (FNP)
7) United Black Nationalists of America (UBNA)
8) The New Pan-African Movement (TNPAM)
9) Southern Christian Leadership Conf. (SCLC)
10) The National Urban League (NUL)
11) Natl. Assoc. for the Advancement of Colored People (NAACP)
12) Committee on Racial and Religious Progress (CORARP)

Note:
At the appropriate time, to be designated by the President, the leaders of some of these organizations are to be detained ONLY WHEN IT IS CLEAR THAT THEY CANNOT PREVENT THE EMERGENCY, working with local public officials during the first critical hours. All other leaders are to be detained at once. Compiled lists of Minority leaders have been readied at the National Data Computer Center. It is necessary to use the Minority leaders designated by the President in much the same manner in which we use Minority members who are agents with CENTRAL and FEDERAL, and we cannot, until there is no alternative, reveal KING ALFRED in all of its aspects. Minority members of Congress will be unseated at once. This move is not without precedent in American history.

Preliminary Memo: Department of Defense
This memo is being submitted in lieu of a full report from the Joint Chiefs of Staff. That report is now in preparation. There will be many cities where the Minority will be able to put into the street a superior number of people with a desperate and dangerous will. He will be a formidable enemy, for he is bound to the continent by heritage and knows that political asylum will not be available to him in other countries. The greatest concentration of the Minority is in the Deep South, the Eastern seaboard, the Great Lakes Region and the West Coast. While the national population exceeds that of the Minority by more than ten times, we

must realistically take into account the following:

1) An estimated 40-50 percent of the white population will not, for various reasons, engage the Minority during an Emergency.

2) American Armed Forces are spread around the world. A breakout of war abroad means fewer troops at home to handle the Emergency.

3) Local law enforcement officials must contain the Emergency until help arrives, though it may mean fighting a superior force.

New York City, for example, has a 25,000 man police force, but there are about one million Minority members in the city. We are confident that the Minority could hold any city it took for only a few hours. The lack of weapons, facilities, logistics---all put the Minority at a final disadvantage.

Since the Korean War, this Department has shifted Minority members of the Armed Forces to areas where combat is most likely to occur, with the aim of eliminating, through combat, as many combat-trained Minority servicemen as possible. Today the ratio of Minority member combat deaths in Vietnam, where they are serving as "advisors," is twice as high as the Minority population ration to the rest of America.

Below is the timetable for KING ALFRED as tentatively suggested by the JCS who recommended that the operation be made over a period of eight hours. Countdown to eight hours begins the moment the President determines the Emergency to be:
- A) National
- B) Coordinated
- C) Of Long Duration

8th Hour - Local police and Minority leaders in action to head off the Emergency.

7th Hour - County Police join Local police

6th Hour - State Police join county & local forces

5th Hour - Federal Marshals join state, county and local forces.

4th Hour - National Guards federalized, held in readiness.

3rd Hour - Regular Armed Forces alerted to take up positions. Minority troops divided, and detained, along with white sympathizers, under guard.

2nd Hour - All Minority leaders, national and local detained.

1st Hour - President addresses the Minority on radio-television, gives it one hour to end the Emergency.

0 - All units under regional commands into the Emergency.

"O" Committee Report:

Survey shows that, during a six-year period, Production created 9,000,000 objects, or 1,500,000 each year. Production could not dispose of the containers, which provided a bottleneck. However, that was almost 20 years ago. We suggest that vaporization techniques be employed to overcome the Production problems inherent in KING ALFRED.

-END-
This is the end of the KING ALFRED document.

We know, that there are many of us, who will refuse to believe or accept this document as authentic. Some think that America is too modern or too civilized to round up people they consider as being verbally or physically dangerous to their ideas or methods of rulership. All subversives, revolutionaries and those considered as enemies of the state (USA), will be collected and detained. This has happened many times around the world and right here in America.

We can be sure that there is some variation of the KING ALFRED PLAN currently on file in Washington, D.C., we saw a glimpse of it during the Civil Rights Marches in Memphis and other places. If a situation arises that even remotely resembles a national rioting problem from the Minority population - a plan will be put into effect to militarily round up us and put us into what can be called "Concentration Camps." Families will be split up, our men, women and children will be separated and put into what will be called "Detainment Centers," instead of "Concentration Camps." These camps have been readied since World War II in 1943. This action is not unprecedented for use on red, yellow or Black people right here in America. The laws still exist.

This year's televised evacuation of the citizens of KOSOVO, in central Europe, due North of Africa,, bordered by the Mediterranean Sea, provides a good demonstration of what the evacuation of a city of almost one-million people looks like. We have seen men, women and children, sick and well, walking on foot, carrying packages, fleeing with only the clothes on their back, scrambling for food and lining up in front of water trucks - all during the cold of winter. This forced exodus of the Albanian people, allegedly based on ethnic cleansing, gives a true picture of the frustration, demoralization, desperation and helplessness experienced by people who are militarily suppressed and prodded from one place to another - on foot. In KOSOVO only a small number of lives have been taken (as of the writing of this book), and yet NATO (North Atlantic Treaty Organization) and the U.N. (United Nations), and the U.S. A. are all in agreement to bomb the offending country and try to remove it's government. Air Forces and troops from all over the world have come to the aid of these Albanian refugees. America has already committed to take in over 20,000 Albanians and give them asylum. War tactics and a personal invitation to come to America, has been extended to them based on what the government and NATO is calling a "humanitarian effort." A show of compassion. NATO is made up of about 19 Democracies from around the world. We are in a country which is currently throwing poor people (American citizens) off the welfare claiming they can no longer afford to carry them and support their children. And while NATO and the UN (including the USA which has spent over $150 Million), are sending dollars to these white people, transporting them to Guam, and provide them with food, clothing and shelter; but none of these international organizations lifted a finger to help the people of Rwanda (Rowanda) located deep in Africa back in 1994 when over a million Black Africans were murdered, with others forced to leave their homes and flee for their safety. The same type of "human suffering" existed, and we saw visual proof on television of what happening to the people there too, but no one came to their aid. There also was no "humanitarian effort," or "Operation Sustain Hope," shown to the Black Africans killed in Nigeria. There was no NATO, UN or USA military intervention in Rowanda or Nigeria. It seems as if the U.S.A., NATO and the U.N. are only interested in defending white people in areas which help stabilize America financially or politically. Africa is not important to them, and in the final analysis, neither are we, as African-

Americans. There is no one to come to our aid from a foreign land. Aside from the fact that other countries will be dealing with their own problems, there is no foreign government willing to take on the USA in a military fight - especially over us. We are not needed. We are dispensable dependents. So it is not out of the question that we too could be rounded us and detained in a place of their designation. They have laws to cover everything they want to do against anybody anywhere. The KING ALFRED Plan is just an example.

We already have a similar program called: "MARTIAL LAW," which is sanctioned under the FEMA program, Federal Emergency Management Act. Originally sanctioned by John F. Kennedy, as Executive Order #10997, "Assigning Emergency Preparedness Functions to the Secretary of the Interior," written in 1962, the scope of this order was" The Secretary of the Interior, shall prepare national emergency plans and develop preparedness programs covering (1) electric power; (2) petroleum and gas; (3) solid fuels; and (4) minerals. These plans and programs shall be designed to provide a state of readiness in these resource areas with respect to all conditions of national emergency, including attack upon the United States. Reorganization Plan No. 1 of 1958 (72 Stat. 1799). Both signed during the Civil Rights era, the next Executive Order #10998 "Assigning Emergency Preparedness Functions to the Secretary of Agriculture." Scope: The Secretary of Agriculture shall prepare national emergency plans and develop preparedness programs covering: Food resources, farm equipment, fertilizer, and food resource facilities, rural fire control, defense against biological warfare, chemical warfare, and radiological fallout pertaining to agricultural activities, and rural defense information and education. "Food Resources" here means "all commodities and products, simple, mixed or compound, or complements to such commodities or products, that are capable of being eaten or drunk, by either human beings or animals irrespective of other uses to which such commodities or products may be put, at all stages of processing from the raw commodity to the products thereof in vendible form for human or animal consumption. For the purposes of this order the term 'food resources' shall also include all starches, sugars, vegetable and animal fats and oils, cotton, tobacco, wool, mohair, hemp, flax fiber and naval stores, but shall not include any such material after it loses its identify as an agricultural commodity or agricultural product." This order means that they (the government) can take complete and total control over all the food, and anything that can be used as food, whenever they think the need arises. There are other Executive Orders covering: The Secretary of Energy with respect to all forms of energy, The secretary of Health and Human Services with respect to health resources, The Secretary of Transportation with respect to all forms of civil transportation. The Secretary of Defense with respect to water resources, The secretary of Commerce for all other materials, services and facilities, including construction materials. They have several such orders which when translated say and confirm that they own and control everything.

There is a more recent Executive Order #12919, signed by President William Jefferson Clinton, on June 3, 1994, called the "National Defense Industrial Resources Preparedness." which reads very similar to the FEMA instruction documents, but they include in Part VI - Employment of Personnel, Sec. 601, another para-military instruction noting that "there is established in the Executive Branch a National Defense Executive Reserve (NDER) composed of persons of recognized expertise from various segments of the private sector and from government (except full-time Federal employees), for training for employment in executive positions in the Federal Government in the event of an emergency that requires such employment. The head of any department or agency may establish a unit of the NDER and train members of that unit."

"The director, FEMA, shall coordinate the NDER program activities of departments and agencies in establishing units of the Reserve; provide for appropriate guidance for recruitment, training, and activation, and issue necessary rules and guidance in connection with this program.

Section 602 of this same document reads:

"Consultants. The head of each department or agency assigned functions under this order is delegated authority under sections 710(b) and (c) of the Act to employ persons of outstanding

81

experience and ability without compensation and to employ experts, consultants, or organizations. The authority delegated by this section shall not be redelegated."

This translates to mean that the Government can pick up any of us they choose, according to our qualifications, and force us to help them do whatever they're doing -with no choice and NO PAY. As in slave labor. In Part IX - General Provisions, Section 901 (a), "Civil Transportation includes movement of persons and property by all modes of transportation in interstate, intrastate, or foreign commerce within the United States, its territories and possessions, and the District of Columbia, and, without limitation, related public storage and warehousing, ports, services, equipment and facilities, such as transportation carrier shop and repair facilities. Civil transportation shall include direction, control and coordination of civil transportation regardless of ownership. *Translated this means that the government can commandeer your car, van, jeep or truck, and do whatever they want to with it, for as long as they want to.* Section J says: "Health resources means materials, facilities, health supplies and equipment (including pharmaceutical, blood collecting and dispensing supplies, biological, surgical textiles, and emergency surgical instruments and supplies) required to prevent the impairment of, improve, or restore the physical and mental health conditions of the population." Section M reads "Water resources, means all usable water, from all sources, within the jurisdiction of the United States, which can

be managed, controlled, and allocated to meet emergency requirements."
In view of any existing national emergency, the government has complete authority under their laws to come into our homes and demand (take), our food, water, supplies and equipment." This is why it is so important to buy your food now before the panic begins and everybody else is crowding into every store every where. The above described Executive Orders may sound like a bunch of gobbledygook doublespeak, but they contain very pertinent information on our rights as citizens - all the way down to our food, water and car.

CONCENTRATION CAMPS(Detainment Centers):

Many of our people will ignore all warnings about this upcoming world crisis, they will pretend, to the end, that all reports are exaggerated by doomsday prophets, survival food store owners and religious fanatics to gain popularity or make money. Others will be genuinely so traumatized by the situation that they too will become stagnated and so frozen with fear that they will do nothing to prepare. Some of us will throw public tantrums, riot and burn down their neighborhoods in protest against the government for letting them down, not providing for them and abandoning them in their greatest time of need. They will demand that the government help them. For these people the government already has an emergency program designed to round them up, take them in, and to do it under the pretense of program designed to round them up, take them in, and to do it under the pretense of providing for them. The majority of our people will accept this invitation, especially if their block or neighborhood has been gutted with fire and/or disease and pestilence surrounds them as a result of raw sewage flowing in the streets. Some will go voluntarily, others will reject the offer and have to be forced. The military branch initially in charge of rounding up Blacks, Latinos, Asians and Native-Americans, will be the National Guard. There are many Black men and women enlisted in the National Guard and other branches of military service - including police officers. They will either be brainwashed into helping with this task, or they will refuse to participate in this dastardly deed and be arrested and detained themselves. Many minorities will find that no matter how long they have worked in the system and dedicated themselves to law abidance, voting, going to church, and obeying all the rules of America; all of this will be discounted - and the population will be separated by race and class. Dedicated slaves will receive no special recognition or treatment. Tribes will re-convene.

LOCATION OF DETAINMENT CENTERS

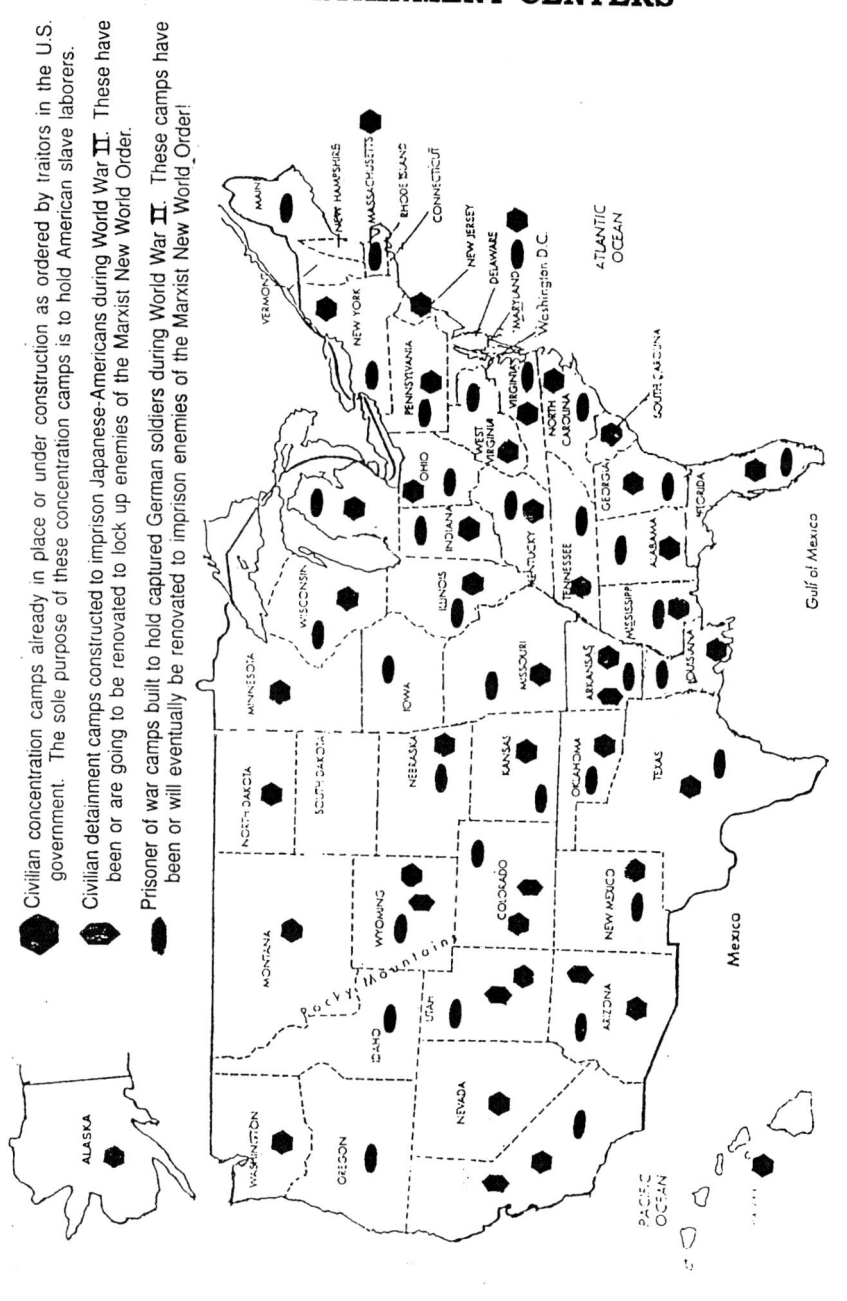

⬢ Civilian concentration camps already in place or under construction as ordered by traitors in the U.S. government. The sole purpose of these concentration camps is to hold American slave laborers.

⬣ Civilian detainment camps constructed to imprison Japanese-Americans during World War II. These have been or are going to be renovated to lock up enemies of the Marxist New World Order.

▮ Prisoner of war camps built to hold captured German soldiers during World War II. These camps have been or will eventually be renovated to imprison enemies of the Marxist New World Order!

85

This Detainment Center (Concentration Camp) location chart and Government Reorg. Chart, are both courtesy of 2 books of excellent research about the secret plans the government has to overpower the private citizens of America and take control of their lives and goods. The books are called America Under Siege, and America in Peril, both written by M.W. Jefferson and published by the Freedom & Liberty Foundation in Knoxville, TN.

GOVERNMENT REORGANIZATION ACT:
(Compare this Map with the King Alfred Plan

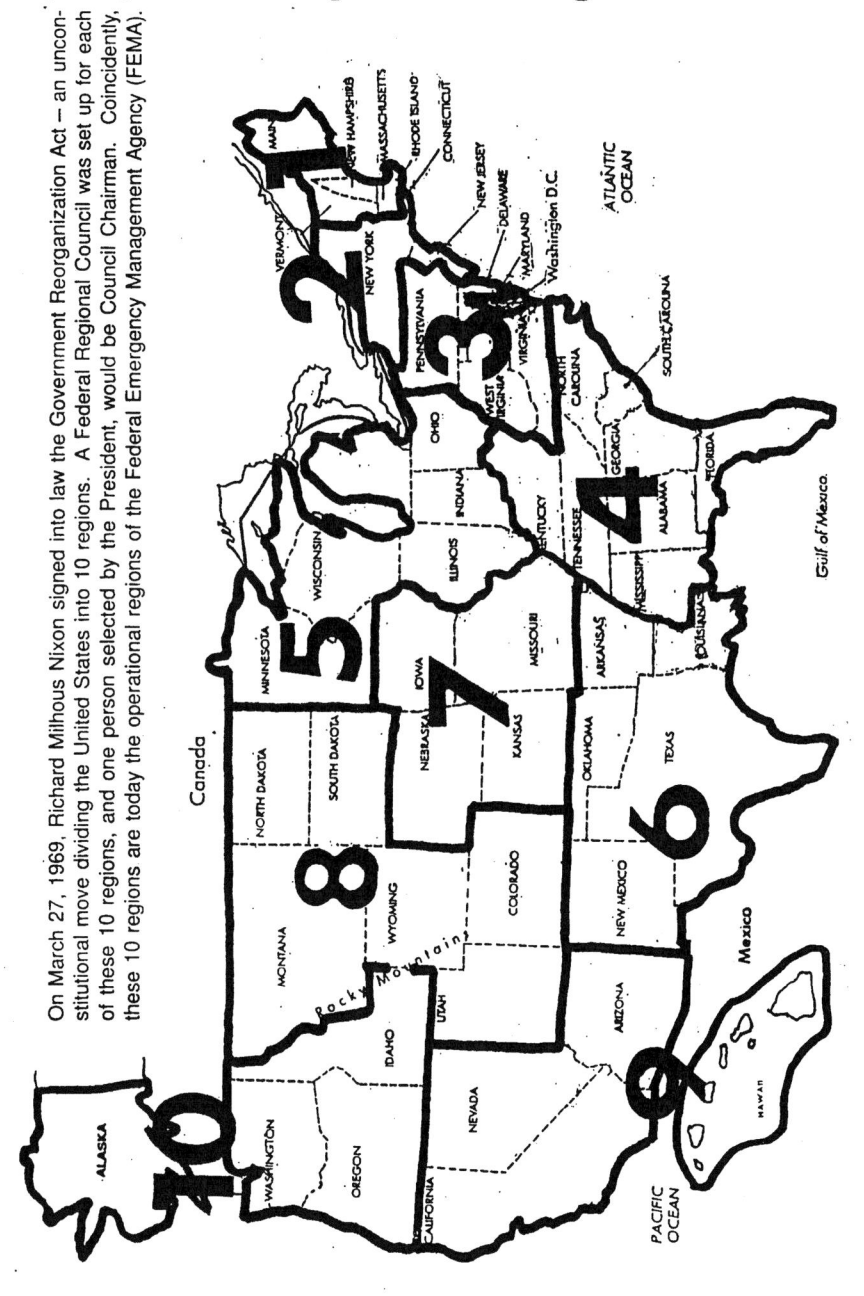

On March 27, 1969, Richard Milhous Nixon signed into law the Government Reorganization Act — an unconstitutional move dividing the United States into 10 regions. A Federal Regional Council was set up for each of these 10 regions, and one person selected by the President, would be Council Chairman. Coincidently, these 10 regions are today the operational regions of the Federal Emergency Management Agency (FEMA).

AN OPEN LETTER TO PEOPLE OF COLOR IN AMERICA:

Dear Black, Sisters and Brothers:

Although we have a natural penchant to love everyone but ourselves, the time is quickly approaching when every race in America will only look out for their own kind. We have endured much pain and torture here in this country and we know now that the body heals much quicker than the mind.

Our time here has been both a blessing and a curse. The blessing is the immense freedom of idea we have in this country. The curse is that in order to participate in America we must reject ourselves. We have become accustomed to either forgetting, or disregarding, the majority of the standards and values practiced by our ancestors. Some of these values we have abandoned out of a sincere desire to blend in, assimilate and meld with our current environment. Our rich and sacrificial heritage's have been, for the most part, put aside, and replaced with American ideas and tolerances. We have mimicked every European style and posture. And in the final analysis we have each tried to make the best of what we have been allowed to have. But we ought not ever forget that we are all here by permission, not right. This is not our homeland, and this is not our culture or history. We are in a land, entrusted to people, who enslaved some of us, illegally imprisoned some of us, attempted genocide on some of us, and forced others into servitude. We are in a land built on the bloody foundation of the Red man, who was unconditionally murdered in order to rob him of his property. We are in a land where the Black man was unmercifully robbed of his culture, and beaten and brainwashed into being a semi-permanent slave. Our well ingrained and deeply religious upbringing, and every spiritual text we honor; concludes for us, that America and her notions cannot thrive because her birthcanal is paved with the pain and disregard of us. Her very premise is against the will of God. All the Gods. We have not produced a God who would be in agreement with America's treatment towards our ancestors. And while many of us feel we are better off here than anywhere else, the price has been high. The cost is one of ongoing duration, each year eliminating more and more of our vast and vibrant histories. If the situation and breakdown causes a short or long interruption of basic life sustaining services; we had *better* be ready. Ready to take a greater responsibility for our survival until this crisis is over, if ever. Joining back on to our roots is the only way to ensure our ultimate survival and sanity. When we do this we will all embrace peace, sharing and dignity. But if the European Americans return to their roots we can expect bloodshed, terror and suffering. Because theirs is a history and legacy of abusing People of Color for selfish reasons. And the situation created by the fall of American systems will give them cause and reason to act against us again. Again.

CONCLUSION

Consider this book a weather forecast. There is a massive storm approaching headed directly towards us mentally dead. This problem is not something we should ignore. This is the time when you must have confidence in yourself and faith in your God.
It will be time to walk it like we talk it, and see what the so-called "conscious community" does. It has always been said that we are a crisis-oriented group, failing to act until the very last moment. If we wait until the very last moment we will be left out, naked, hungry and out of doors. We spend over $800 Billion a year on all sorts of unnecessary and recreational items. We have never prepared for any emergency situation, such as a storm, for more than a few days. Being prepared is no longer have a flashlight, a few candles and extra milk. This time we need to gather all the items we need for basic survival. Don't procrastinate thinking that you can get what you need at the last minute. We do not have that kind of control over materials and goods. We are totally dependent upon the store houses of others to get what we need. When the time comes, your money will not do you any good if you do not already have what you need for you and your family to survive. This will be a time of hard choices, this will be a time of great suffering and doing-without. We need a workable plan. We must be organized and ready. Ready to do-for-self.
All sport and play will be suspended indefinitely. And this alone will create extra stress on us. We

cannot neglect the potential for harsh weather or the influence of the Creator. Do not become embarrassed or discouraged if others laugh at you for preparing for hell. Also do not be tricked by the newspapers and other media if they fail to mention anything about it at all. You must look for the hidden meaning of symbols. There is already proof of the seriousness of this problem. Many of us, for many years, have honored our enslaved ancestors and praised them for their personal strength and fortitude in the middle passage, and for surviving the terrors of early slavery and afterwards. It is their strength we must call upon, it is their sacrifice we must remember in order to get thru this ordeal. You will not be able to convince all of your friends or loved ones, no matter how much you warn them, but you cannot let this deter you from preparing for the worst, while hoping for the best. The streets will be like a fountain of dripping blood. Store up food, make a First-Aid kit, get sleeping bags and extra blankets, get water purification tablets, get plastic bags for human waste, have an alternative place to escape to, stock up on warm clothes, get a short-wave radio. "Survival is through different aspects of light that has been given out; Wisdom, Knowledge and light has been given to fit any and all occasions that would prevail itself at any given time; to recognize different segments of time has been given. If one fails to recognize it before it is upon you, it is one's own fault. There is no amount of pity given out only total suffering when the time has been appointed this happens individually and collectively due to certain circumstances prevailing." Everything you assemble is useful and can be incorporated into your daily life. We need to have these things on hand anyway. We have taken so much for-granted. The next time you take a shower or bath, look at the running water, think about how we blindly expect the water to come on everytime we turn the handle. Think about all the food we waste daily, and all the financial excesses we indulge ourselves in. It may all come to a screeching halt.

We can only do our best. We have tried to do our best every since we were brought here against our will over 400 years ago. We mostly agree that we are/have been in hell here in America. Now this hell is threatened. "Hell is built upon imperfectness, or it would not be considered as Hell. Things are only right to a certain extent, due to the people who constructed it, having imperfect capabilities." We realize that in a situation like this, without divine intervention not a one of us will be saved.

Sadly as a result of the recent political decision we are experiencing the "post-election-blues." We are apprehensive about what the future holds under the rulership of a leader who expresses his desire take things back to old-time-America. We fear losing the so-called racial progress we marched and begged for over the past 65 years. Even some white people are concerned – all worried that new directives will affect our housing, health care, wages, jobs, credit, food and police authority. This little book will help fortify us against the·possible hard-times coming our way. **WE BEST BE READY...**